Old Fyvie
Helen Taylor

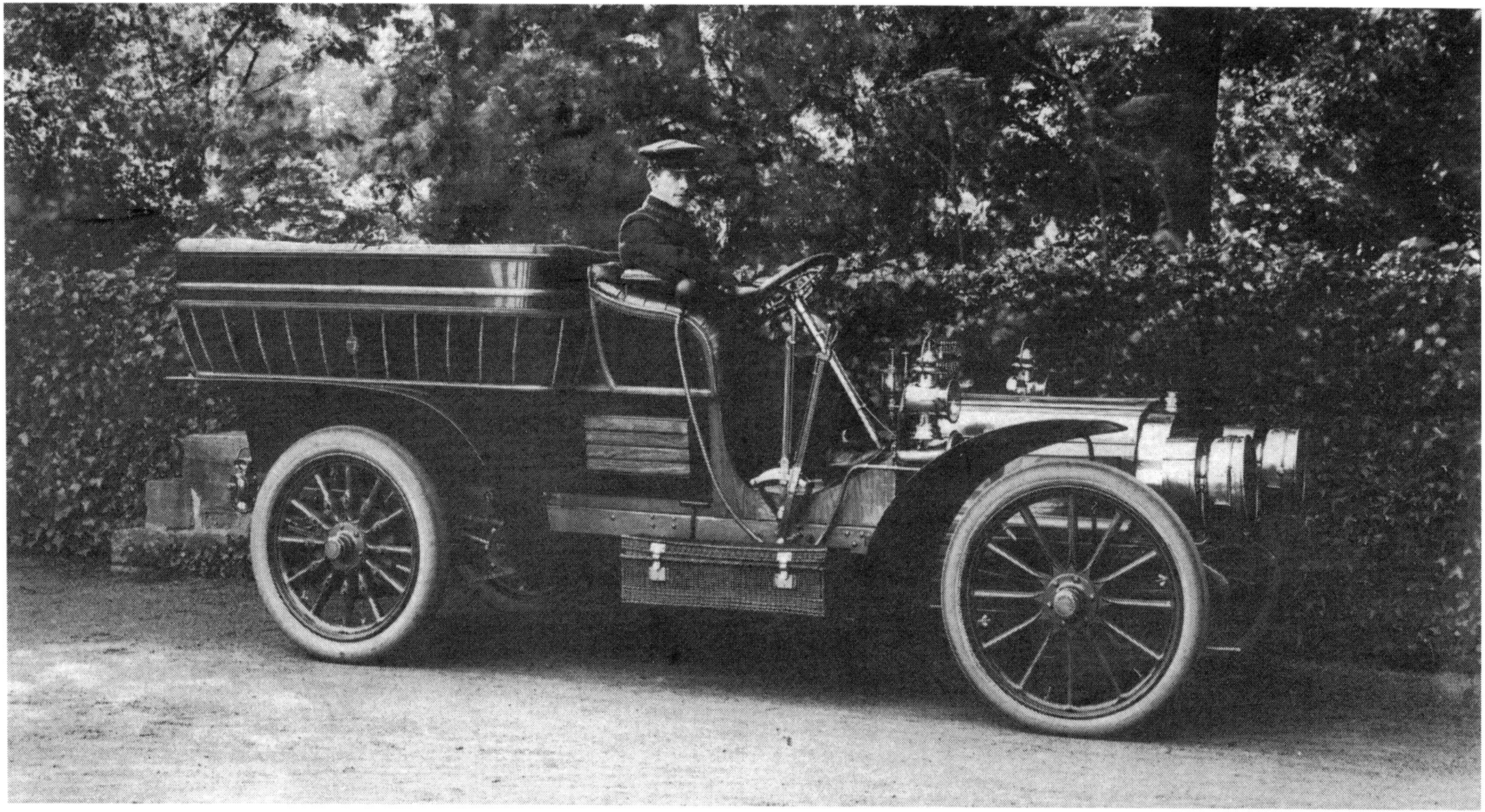

A Léon Bollée car with a custom-built body. In 1906 the King of Spain and his new bride, Princess Victoria of Battenberg, a granddaughter of Queen Victoria, spent part of their honeymoon at Fyvie Castle and were photographed in this car.

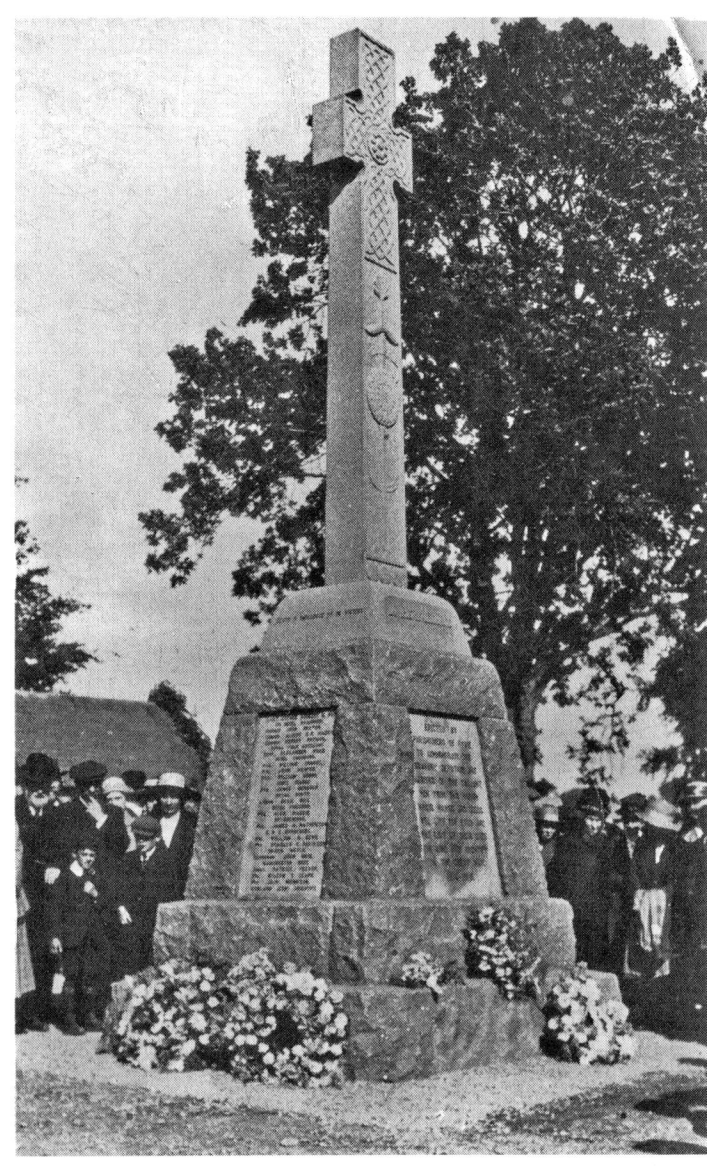

© Helen Taylor, 2023
First published in the United Kingdom, 2023,
by Stenlake Publishing Ltd.
www.stenlake.co.uk
ISBN 978-1-84033-950-5

The publishers regret that they cannot supply
copies of any pictures featured in this book.

Printed by
P2D Books, 1 Newlands Rd,
Westoning, Bedford, MK45 5LD

ACKNOWLEDGEMENTS

I would like to thank Andrew Collins, Carole Eddie and Arthur Groves from Fyvie Heritage, and Mrs William Ferguson, Rothiebrisbane for their assistance in preparing this book. Thanks are also due to Lewis Hutton, who took my original manuscript and polished it.

BIBLIOGRAPHY and SOURCES

The following are a few of the websites and books that were used in the research for this book.

British Newspaper Archive: www.britishnewspaperarchive.co.uk
National Library of Scotland map images: maps.nls.uk

Statistical Accounts of Scotland, 1791, 1845
Temple, William Rev., *The Thanage of Fermartyn*, 1894
Smith, Alexander, *A New History of Aberdeenshire*, 1875

From the end of the First World War, there was a nationwide effort to honour those who had given their lives. Fyvie's memorial commemorates the 67 servicemen lost from 1914 -1918 including the laird's grandson, 2nd Lieutenant Arthur Burn. The memorial was built by public subscription in the centre of the village using Balmoral granite. In the First World War some 300 men from Fyvie parish enlisted, many of them continuing the local tradition, joining up with the Gordon Highlanders. The Royal British Legion in Fyvie looks after the memorial and the surrounding area. Every year there is a remembrance parade and a wreath laying ceremony.

Introduction

Fyvie sits on the River Ythan, guarding the southern end of a sheltered route through the hills of Formartine. The strategic site meant that it was an obvious place for a castle, which later became a Royal residence. The oldest parts of the castle standing are 13th century but there will have been earlier structures that have now been erased. Fyvie at that time was the political centre of Formartine. To reflect this the settlement became a Royal Burgh. Its location is unknown but was probably centred around the parish church. By the mid-14th century once the castle ceased to be a Royal residence the fortunes of the town waned, its residents dispersed and the Royal Burgh of Fyvie was lost.

During the period of Royal Fyvie a priory was established on the edge of the village, between the parish church and Lewes. The foundation of the priory is unknown but is probably sometime in the late 12th century. The Bishop of Aberdeen gave the churches of Fyvie to the Abbey of Arbroath in 1178, a grant confirmed by King William the Lion of Scotland, who encouraged a priory to be built. Alternatively, Fergus Earl of Buchan is said to have founded it in 1179. A third possibility is that it was established in 1285 by Reginald le Chen who was Baron of Inverugie, and Sheriff of both Inverness and Nairn. The priory was dedicated to St. Mary and was a cell of the Abbey of Arbroath occupied by the same order of Tironensian Benedictine monks. The Scottish Reformation of the 1560s saw the end of the occupation of the priory, and it was left to crumble. By the late 18th century all that was left were the foundations, the cells and offices of the monks forming opposite sides of a courtyard with the church between them making a third wall. By the 19th century all that was gone, and a cross was erected in 1868 to mark the site.

During the Wars of the Three Kingdoms (1639-52 and includes the English Civil War which began in August 1642) the castle became the scene of the Battle of Fyvie. In October 1642 the Duke of Montrose was camped at Fyvie Castle with a Royalist force reported to be 1,500 men and 50 horse. They had been in the field for a long time and were poorly supplied. The larger, fresher, Covenanter army had been raised to end the Royalist cause in Scotland. Led by the Marquis of Argyll it comprised 2,500 foot and 1,000 horse. Fyvie Castle was not designed for gun warfare and sits on the valley floor with high ground to the east providing a vantage point for artillery and firearms. Montrose after assessing its poor defences retreated to the high ground, where he established ditches and earthworks for the coming battle. Which then began on 28th of October. Covenanter forces attacked the hill but failed, and even lost gunpowder in a counter-attack by the Royalists. A further two days of skirmishing took place before the Covenanters, running short of supplies for their horses, retreated. Montrose used the retreat as an opportunity to escape. After Fyvie his army dispersed, so Argyll's objective was apparently successful. However, Montrose had escaped and would return as one of the most brilliant and daring generals for the Royalist cause. It is unknown how many casualties there were, the contemporary reports say almost nothing about the losses.

The lack of a village centre persisted until 1672 when Alexander Seton the Third Earl of Dunfermline established a Burgh of Barony in Fyvie, in what is now Woodhead of Fyvie. A tollbooth and mercat cross were built forming the hub of a new village. With a weekly fair on a Thursday and three larger annual fairs the village began to grow again. It wouldn't last. The Seton family were Jacobites and after the rising in 1689 the castle was siezed by the Crown and the village began to decline again. The fairs became infrequent and the population began to disperse once more.

However, once the Gordon family took posession of the castle in 1726, the decline was reversed. They actively took an interest in developing the estate and improving its productivity which in turn boosted the growth of the village. At this time there were three main centres of the village. Woodhead of Fyvie was on the hill above the river, Kirktown around the parish church, and Lewes on the crossing of the river. The latter had a well known inn, the Lews of Fyvie, that served traffic on the path through the hills. The easy gradients and sheltered nature of the route made it the obvious passage for the turnpike road in 1804 and the railway in 1857. The construction of the road and railway consolidated the village. As the 19th century progressed the village moved west closer to those lines of communication. There it has grown for the last two centuries, in the 20th century seeing significant growth in housing, filling the space between Main Street and St. Peter's Church.

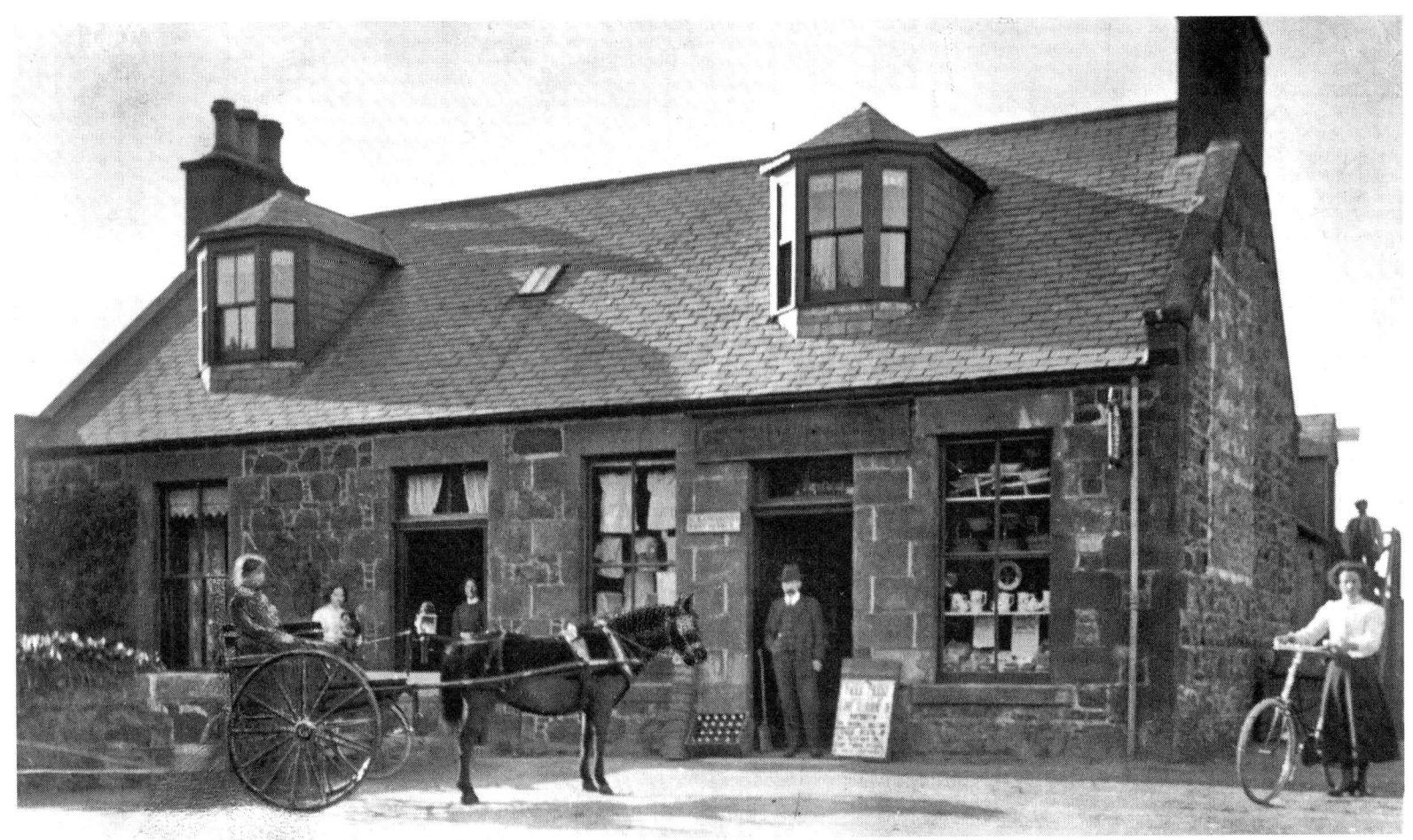

About two miles from Fyvie on the road to Aberdeen, St. Katherines had a shop with post office, a school and schoolhouse. The school was one of seven that served the area. The others were at Steimanhill, Woodhead, Meiklefolla, Fyvie, All Saint's at Woodhead and Fyvie female school. The schools' average attendance in 1881 was 518 pupils. The post office closed in 1974 and the school was converted to a motel in the 1960s and later to a private house. Since then a small cluster of houses has been built in the area.

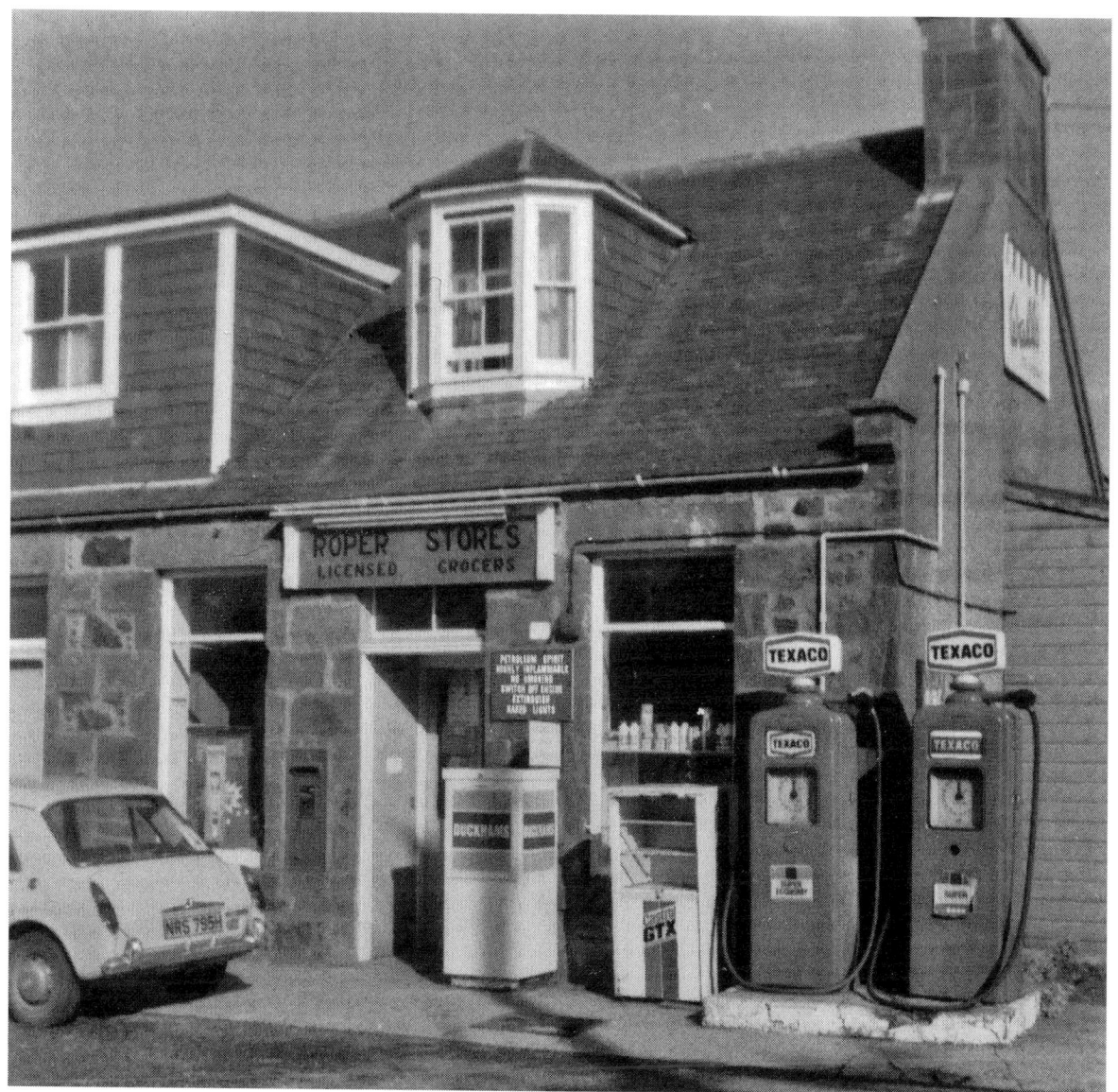

St Katherine's Post Office in September 1974. It also doubled as a petrol station. Between 1946 and his retirement in March 1970 postie Sandy Clark set out on his daily rounds from here. Cycling his 23 mile route delivering post. On hearing of his impending retirement, the mail's grateful recipients organised a presentation in honour of his service to the community. They also successfully petitioned for his work to be recognised officially and he was awarded the Imperial Service Medal in July 1970 at St. Katherines Post Office.

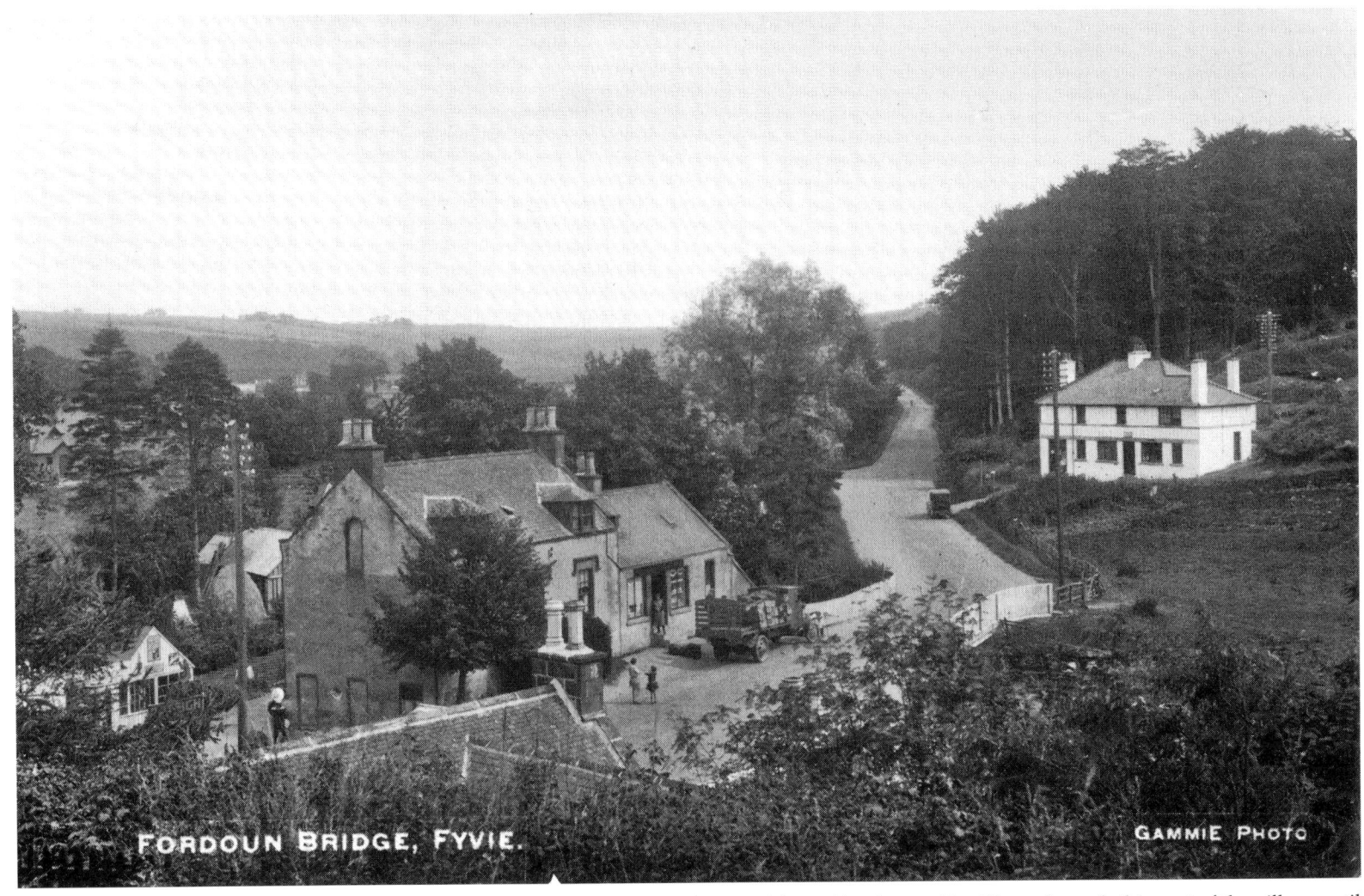

FORDOUN BRIDGE, FYVIE.   GAMMIE PHOTO

The Fordoun Burn joins the River Ythan at the bridge at Lewes, Fyvie. The main road from Aberdeen to Turriff ran through this part of the village until the 1960s when the Fordoun was rerouted and a new road was created bypassing the Howe and cutting the village in half. The lower part of the village had a chemist, bakery, photographer, grocery shop, post office, haberdashery and the old telephone exchange. Fishing for trout was popular at the confluence of the Fordoun and Ythan. Fyvie had an angling association for selling permits and caring for the river.

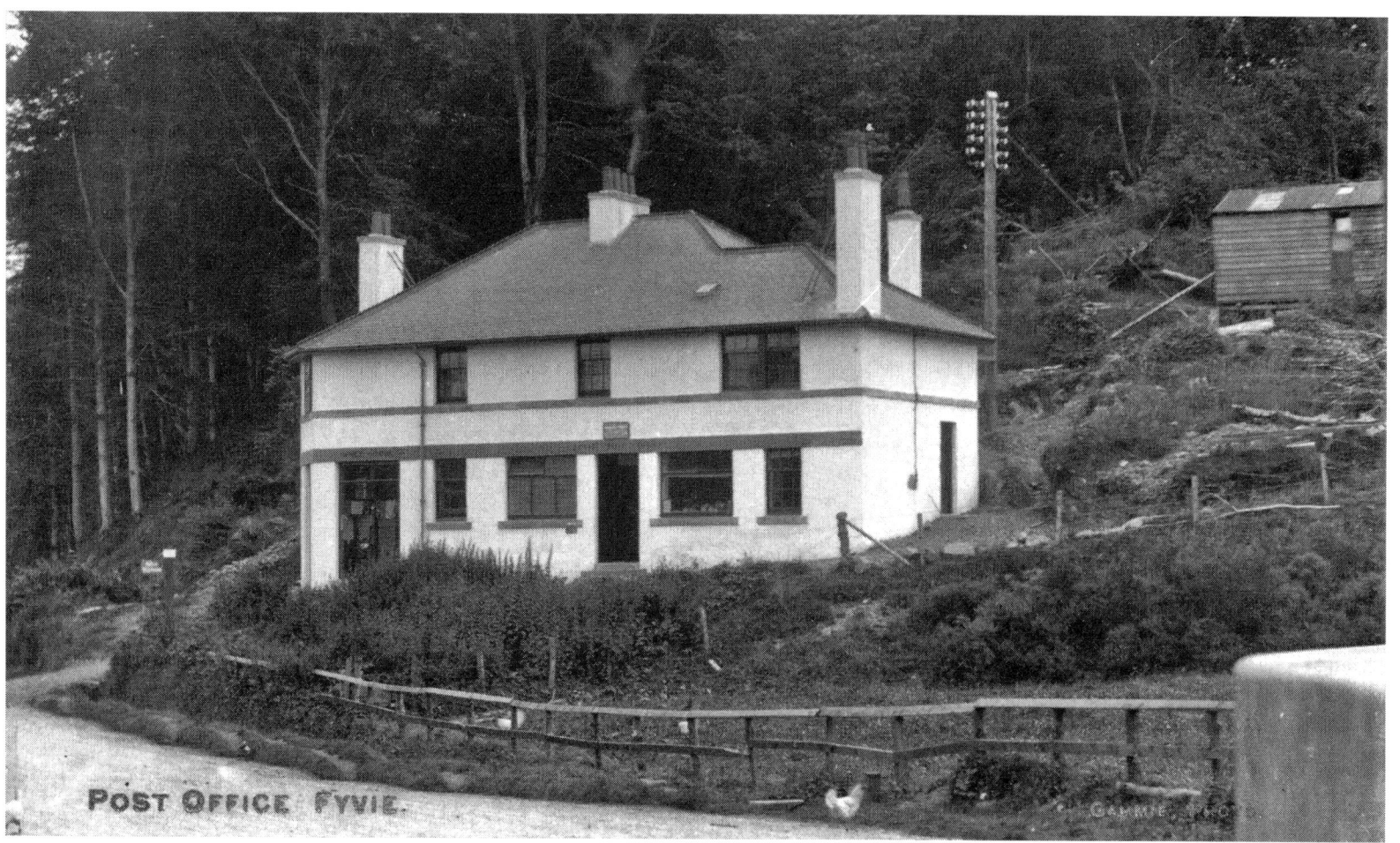

POST OFFICE FYVIE.

Fyvie has a long history as a post town, and is listed in the 'Table of Post Towns in Scotland' contained in the *Edinburgh Almanac* of 1754. With the construction of the Aberdeen to Banff Turnpike in 1804 the toll bar on the road became the village's post office which remained in the Fourdoun Bridge area, its location changing with the post master until 1857 when it moved to the Main Street in Fyvie village. In the early 1920s Fyvie Post Office moved to this building in Fordoun Bridge. It was built to provide both a post office and telephone exchange, facilitating the rapidly expanding telephone services across rural Aberdeenshire in the 1920s, when many combined premises were constructed. At the time, and until 1982, the General Post Office had a monopoly on telephone lines and calls. The photograph is post November 1924 when Miss Minty advertised the opening of her store selling drapery and fancy goods.

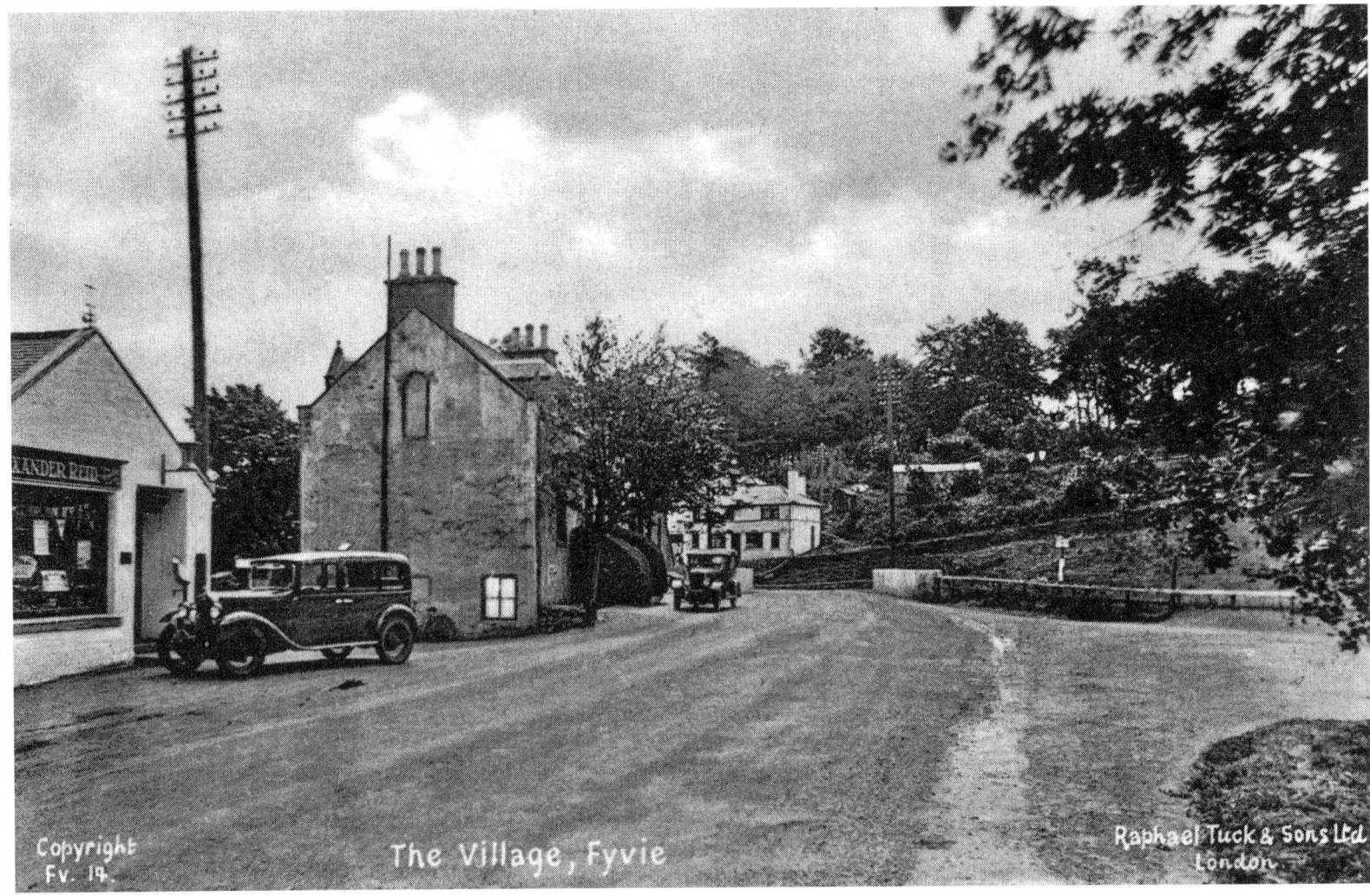

Alexander Reid's, the chemists shop in 1914 with the mortar and pestle above the door. The shop was later owned by Stuart and Alex Todd. The large building is Fordoun House which was part of the Co-op enterprise in Fyvie which had a busy bakery and grocery shop. The main A947 road from Aberdeen to Turriff passed this way until 1975 when the road was realigned and bypassed this area. In 1986 an information centre was opened to cater for visitors to the area and to the recently opened Fyvie Castle.

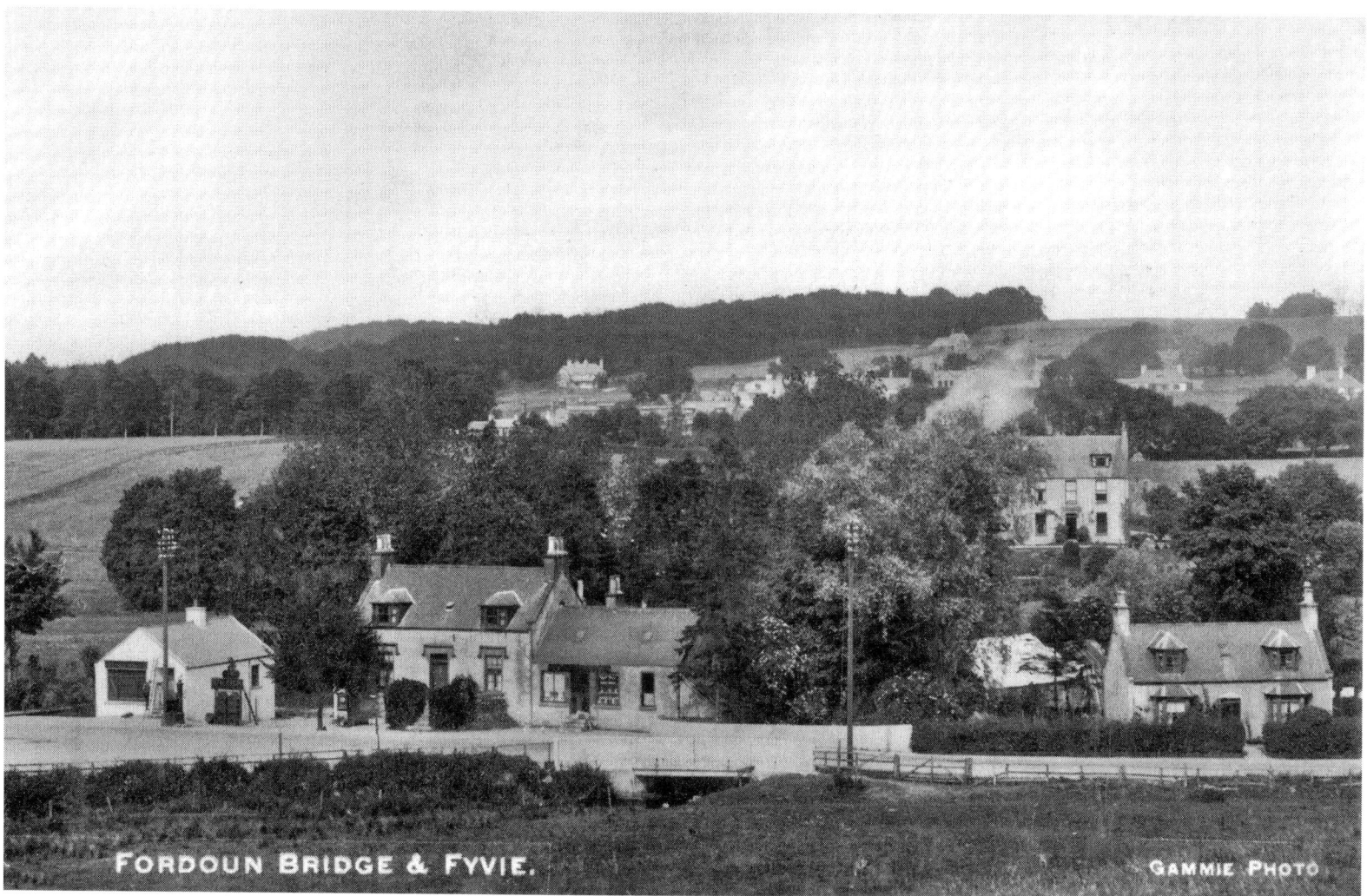

FORDOUN BRIDGE & FYVIE.   GAMMIE PHOTO

The bridge over the Fordoun Burn with Fyvie in the background, probably photographed in the late 1920s. There is a petrol pump and a stand for motor supplies to the right of Alexander Reid's shop and an advert for Raleigh, who for a brief period also produced motorcycles and three wheeled vans in addition to the bicycles they are better known for today. Ironically, Reid was killed in a traffic accident at Fyvie Station in November 1930, clipped by the mudgard of a passing vehicle as he waited to catch a bus home. His wife continued the business until 1936.

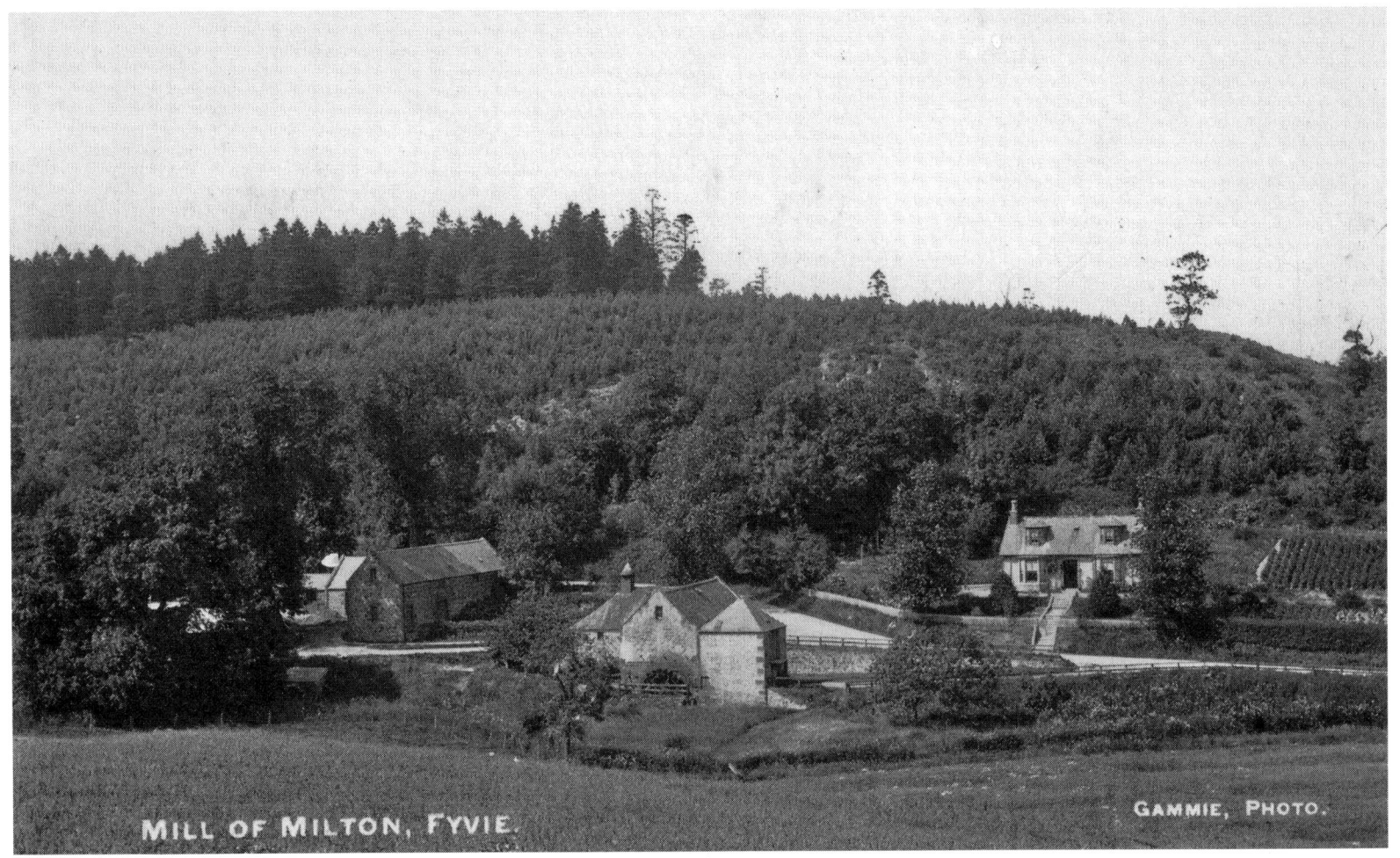

A short distance upstream from the bridge was the Mill of Milton, a meal mill on the burn which forms a dark line in the foreground of the photograph. Not long after this photograph was taken the kiln house, distinguished by its chimney on the left (upstream) side of the mill, burned down. The fire was discovered at about 10.00 pm on 5th February 1930. The miller, John Douglas, who had recently taken over the tenancy of the mill tried to fight the blaze alone. The smoke was so thick and dark that he quickly lost his bearings. If he hadn't stumbled upon the grain chute from the kiln he would probably have suffocated before he reached the door. Helpers were soon on the scene and worked to save the main mill building and its machinery, as well as the stored grain. The kiln house collapsed early in the morning, but through their efforts the main mill was saved only to be demolished in the early 1970s.

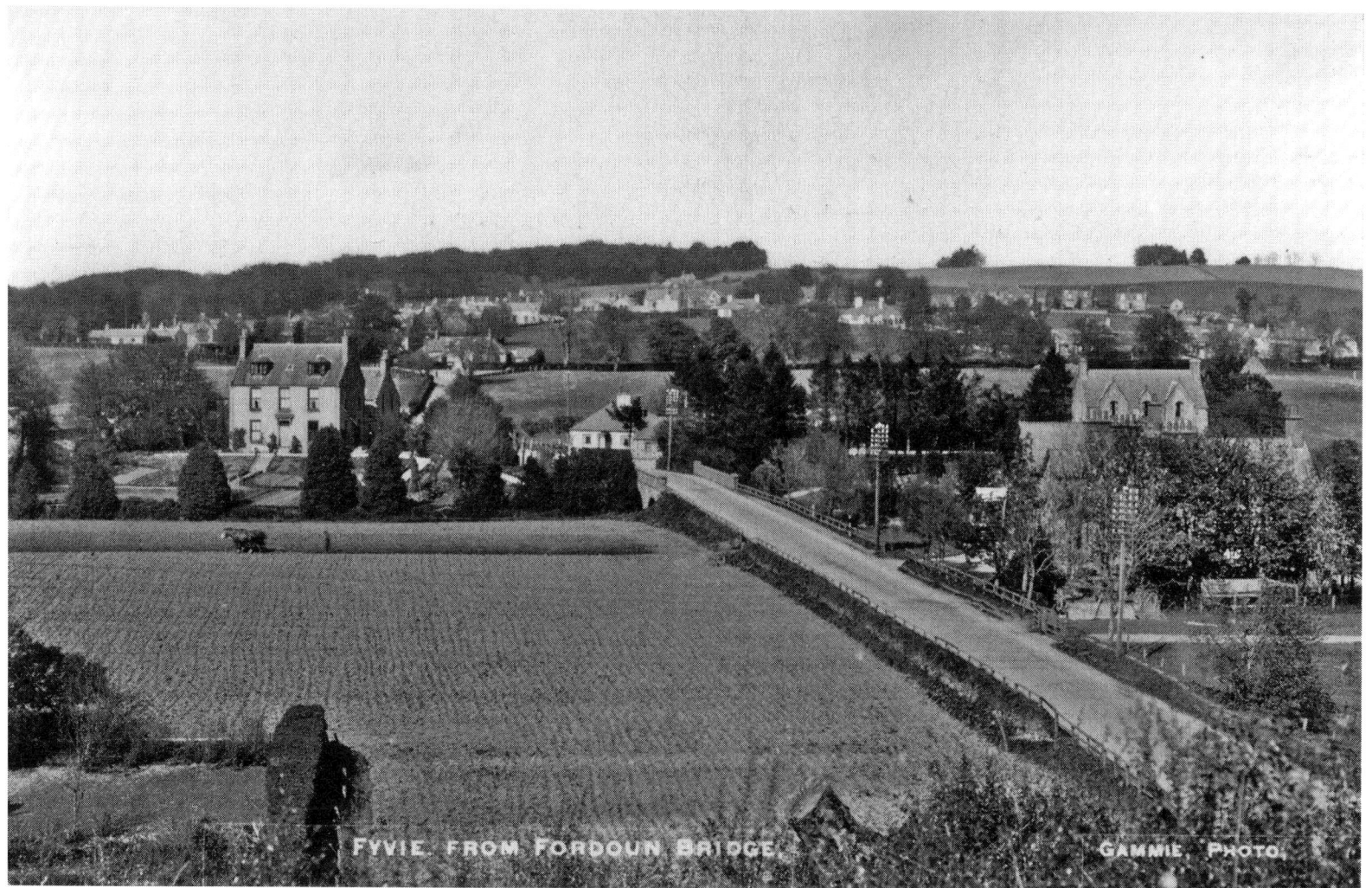

Looking towards Fyvie from Fordoun Bridge. Bank House is prominent on the left with it's gardens sloping down towards the River Ythan. The roof of the Club House, now the Vale Hotel, peaks among the trees on the right. Behind it are the upper floor windows of Ythanside on the other side of the river. In 1898 Mr Mackie of Ythanside was invited to lay a memorial stone for the new bridge seen in the photograph. It was Mrs Forbes Leith who opened it on 5th December that year by cutting a ribbon, before crossing the bridge in a carriage. The bridge has since been upgraded.

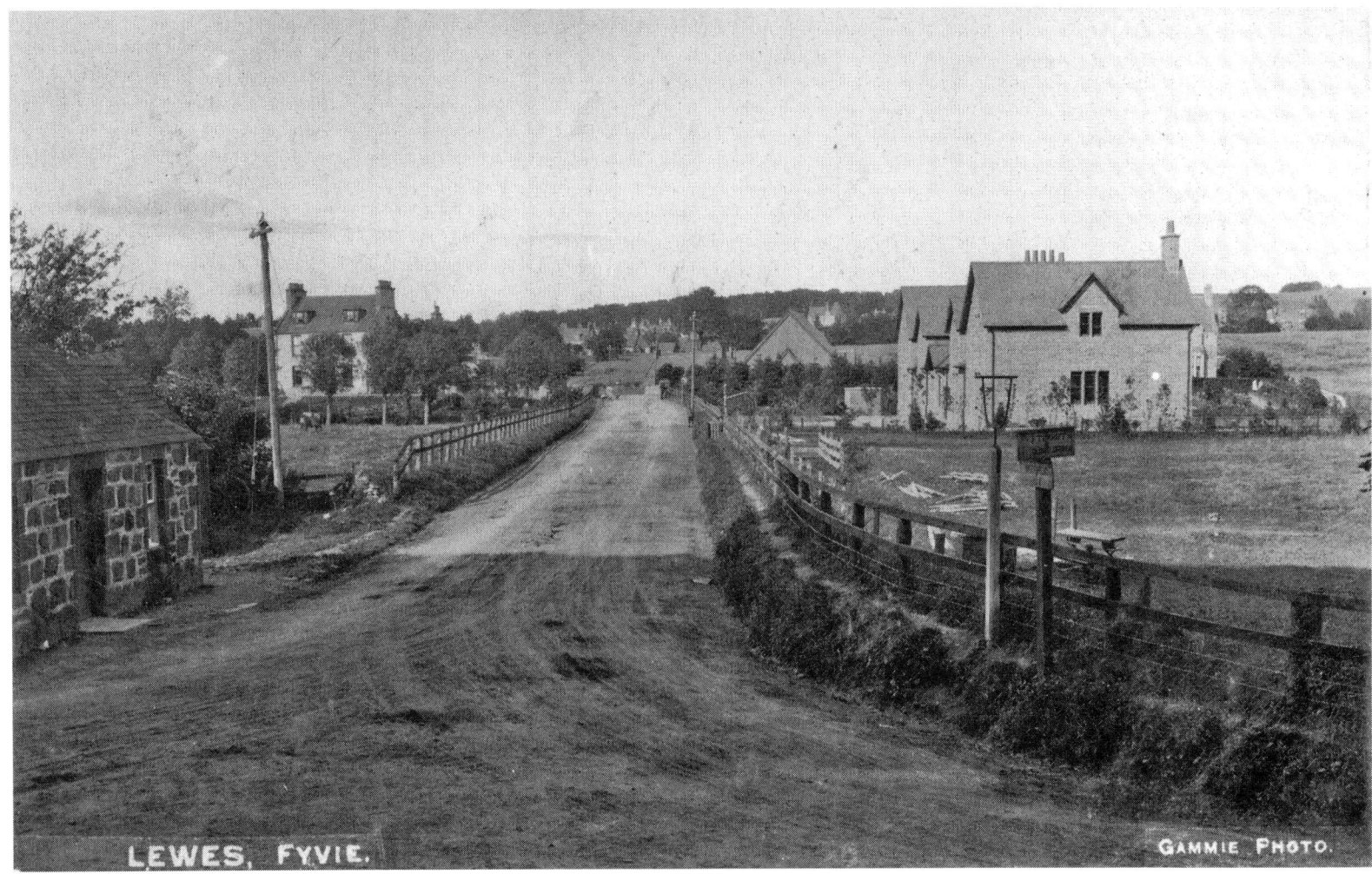

LEWES, FYVIE.   GAMMIE PHOTO.

Looking along the Fyvie road, now the B9005, to the bridge over the Ythan. The building on the left is the old Toll Bar of the Aberdeeen Banff Turnpike. It was built sometime around 1806 and for a while served as the village's post office. The turnpike, which became the A947 in 1922, was considered too narrow and a programme of road widening was begun. In 1926 the Toll Bar was demolished to accommodate the wider road. By the 1960s the 1920s road was considered substandard and a new road was built that bypassed Fordoun Bridge which runs across the fields between the photographer and the Club House of the right.

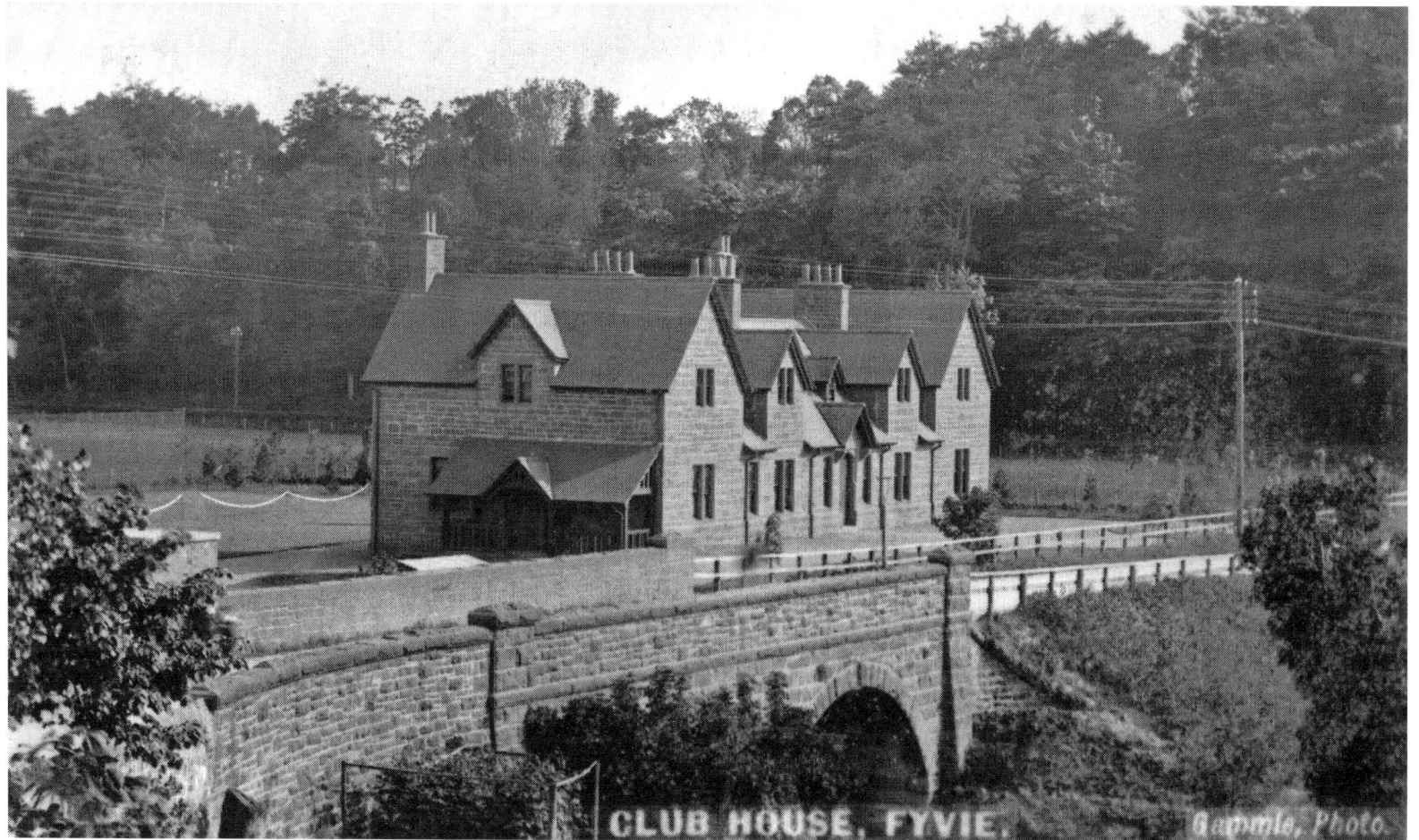

The Club House, Fyvie was built in 1905 as a recreation centre, known as 'The Club'. It was gifted by Lord Leith of Fyvie Castle for self-improvement, recreation and social enjoyment for the people of Fyvie and had tennis courts, lawns, a library, a quiet room for reading or letter writing and a smoking room. It also had acetylene gas lighting and an orchestral organ which was to be powered by water. No gambling was allowed, and subscriptions were five shillings a year. Bed and breakfast was two shillings and sixpence per night. It was used as an auxilliary hospital during the First World War for injured soldiers. There was also a camp for prisoners of war in the surrounding grounds. In its temperance hall weddings were held and it has also been used as a school classroom. It was finally turned into a licensed hotel in the 1960s. Near the entrance stands a pillbox, a Department of Fortifications and Works type 22 built during the Second World War.

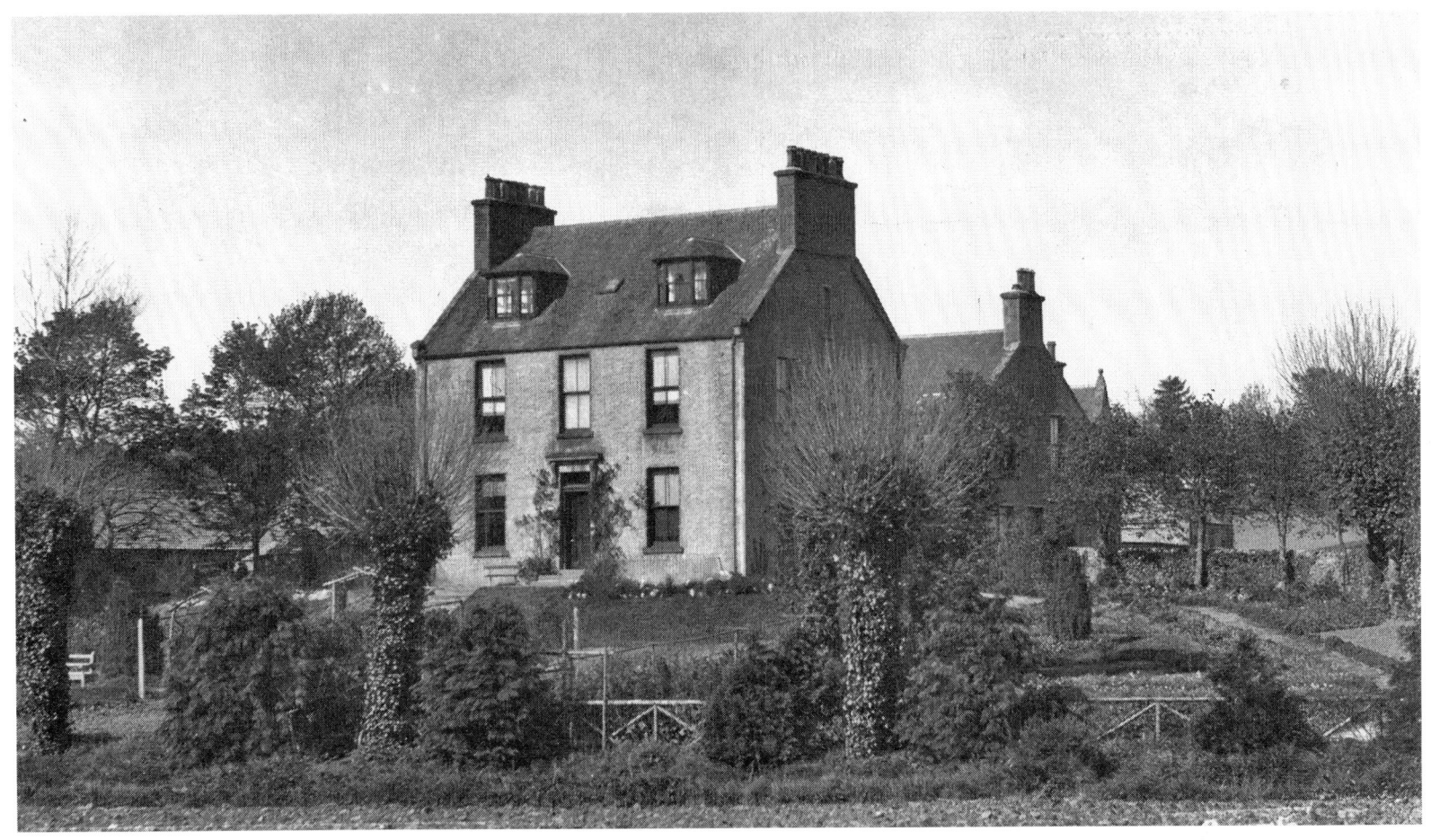

Bank House, seen in the photograph was built in 1866, to the designs of Aberdeen architect James Mathews, to house a branch of the Aberdeen Town and County Bank. The Aberdeen bank was founded in 1825 and by 1831 Adam Mackie of Fyvie was listed among their agents, operating a branch in the village. The Aberdeen Town and County Bank amalgamated with the North of Scotland bank in 1908 and was taken over by the London City and Midland Bank in 1923. They had also bought the Clydesdale Bank three years earlier, but ran their Scottish banks separately until 1950 when they unified them as the Clydesdale Bank. The Fyvie branch continued operating under that name until 2005 when it was closed. The Mackies were also on the board of directors for the Fyvie Savings Bank, established in 1837 to give farm servants, and labourers the opportunity to save and manage money. A local mutual bank, it operated under the umbrella of the village's main bank, but provided a more informal banking environment. It put itself into liquidation on 28th February 1964.

Lewes of Fyvie

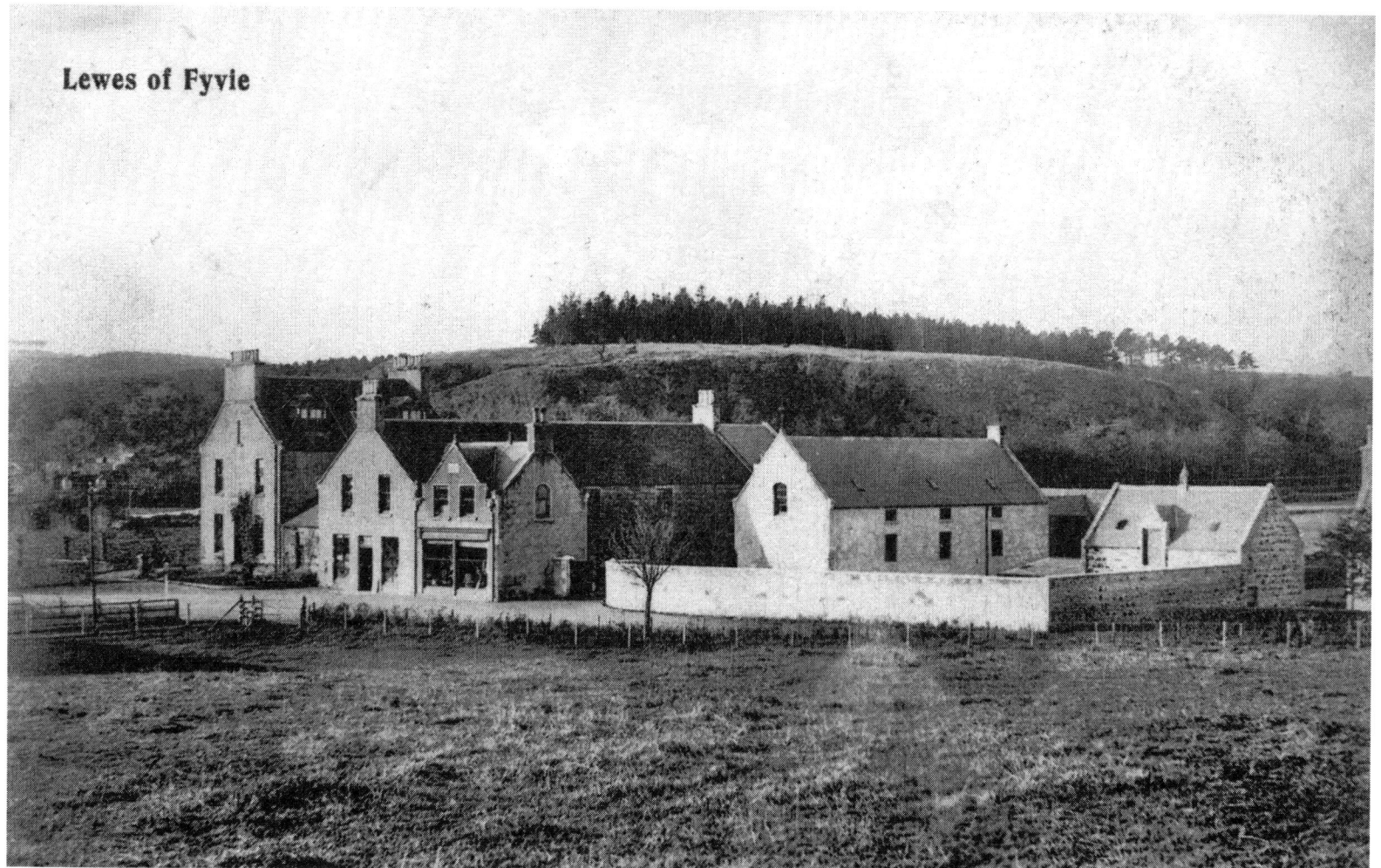

Bank House is on the left in this photo of the shops and warehouses at Lewes of Fyvie. In the 18th century there was an inn called Lews of Fyvie on the site with an adjacent farm – the first account of it is in 1723 described as well established. It was here that Adam Mackie had a shop and proved his mercantile abilities before becoming an agent for the Aberdeen bank. His early diaries have been published as *The Diary of a Canny Man 1818-1828* and provide insight into the beginnings of the Mackie family's association with Lewes of Fyvie. They paid for the construction of the buildings seen here, designed by James Mathews.

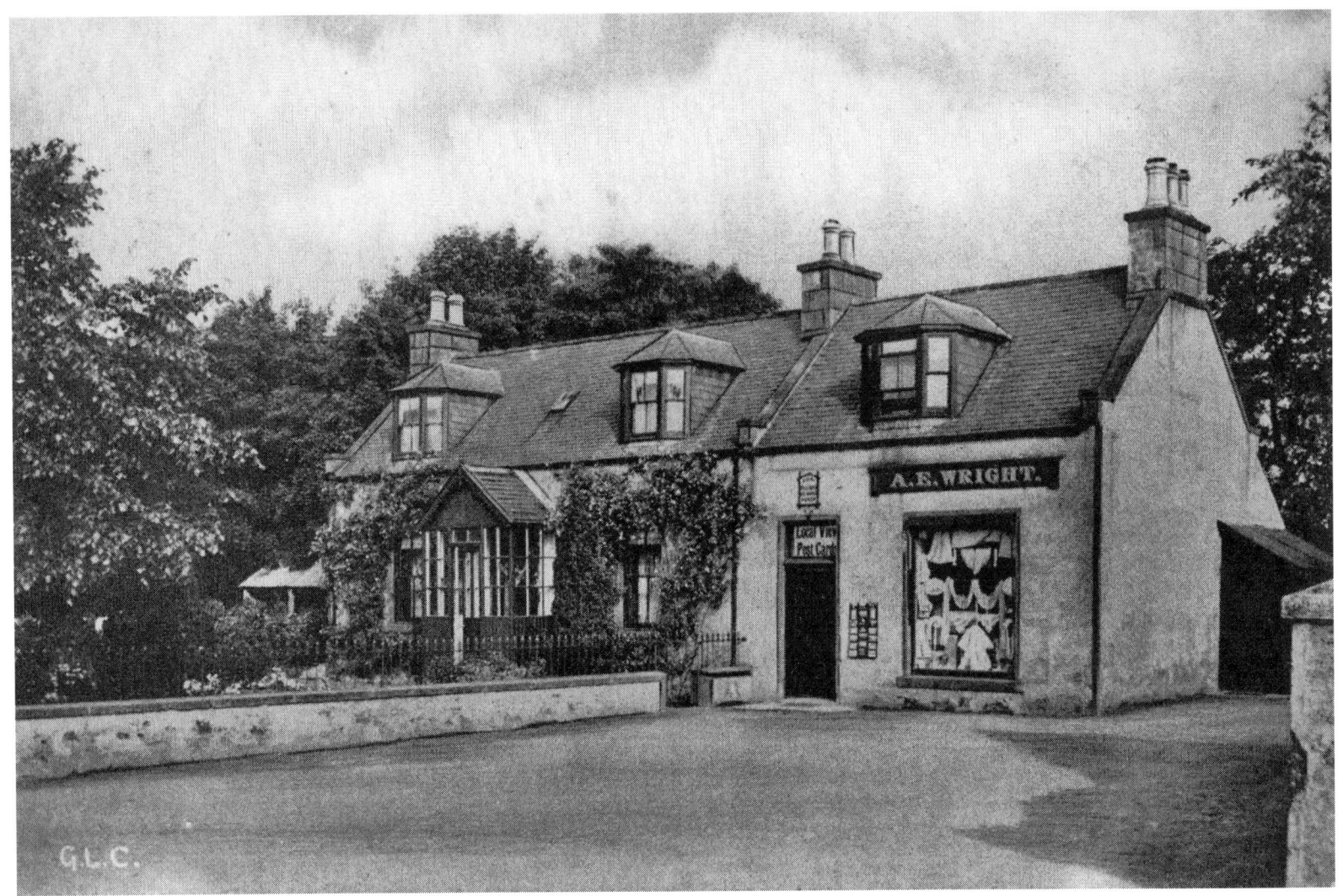

The Grange and A. E. Wright's shop, Main Street. The postcards on sale in the shop, views of Fyvie were taken by a G.L.C. There was George L. Cruickshank who was the village chemist and would have had access to the chemicals required for developing the photos. Alexander Edward Wright was the draper in the village; he died in 1912 aged 47. The house is now known as Norwood and it has an unusual large basement area.

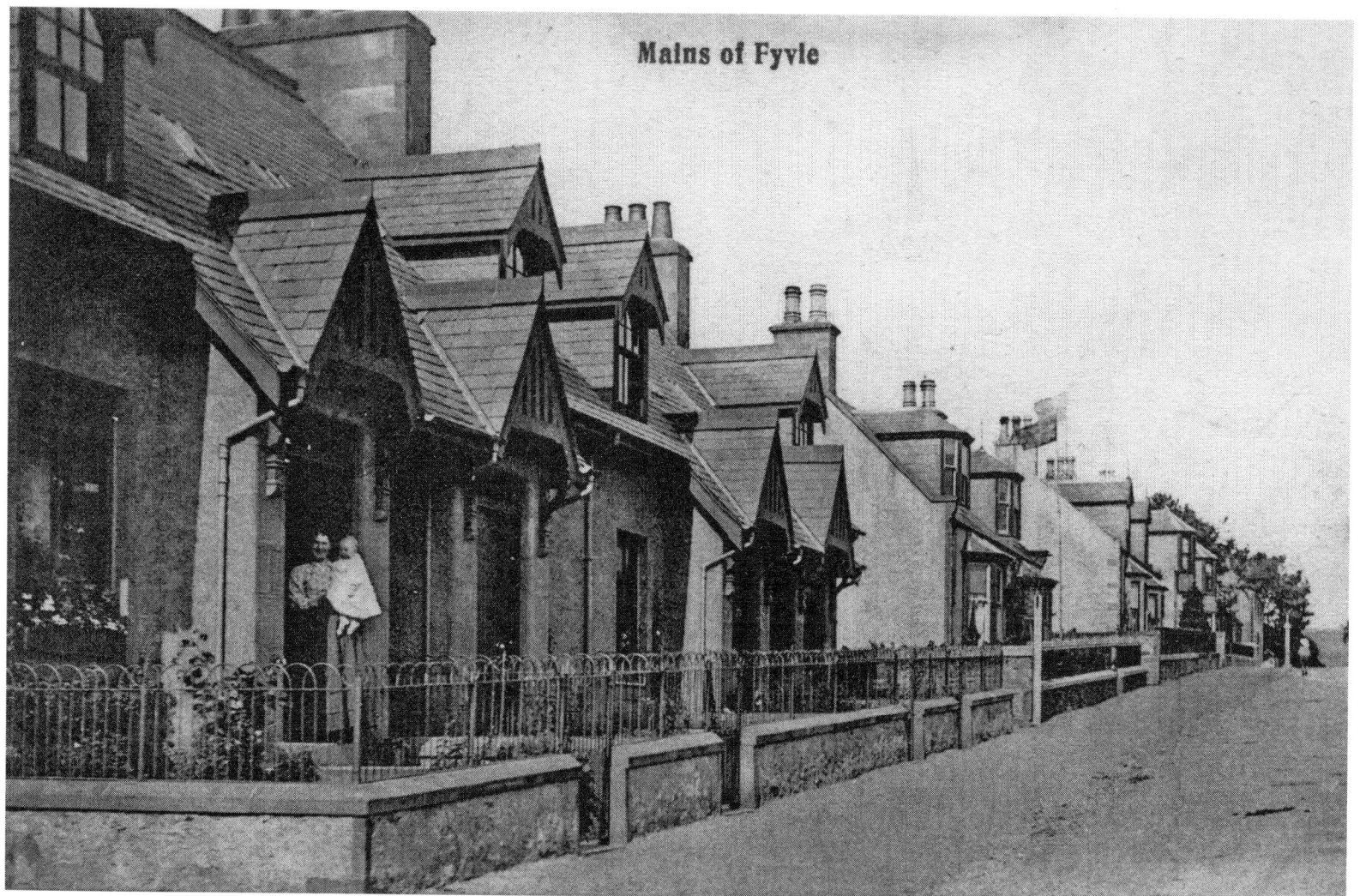

Architect William Liddle Duncan designed several of the cottages and bungalows on Fyvie Main Street, including these ones, the Percy Villas.

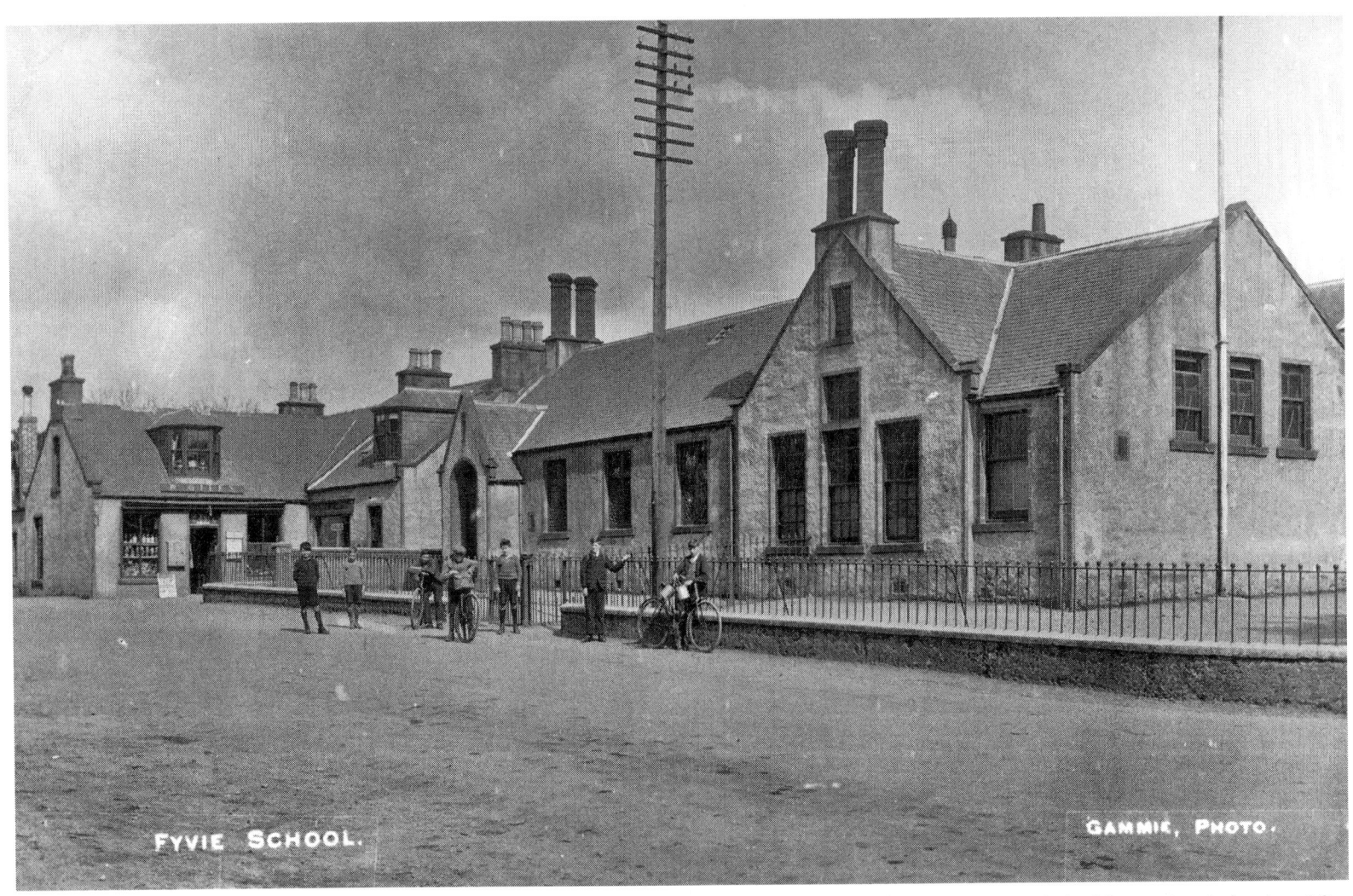

From the late 1890s Fyvie public primary and secondary school was on this site. The classrooms had sloping floors with double wooden desks. A coal fire in the corner of the room provided heat in the colder months. The school had separate playgrounds for boys and girls and an outside toilet block which froze in the wintertime. There was no canteen or hall in the old school. The school taught pupils until they reached fifteen years of age. Subjects included Latin, French, Science and Mathematics. The building was demolished in the 1960s and the Preston House flats built on the site.

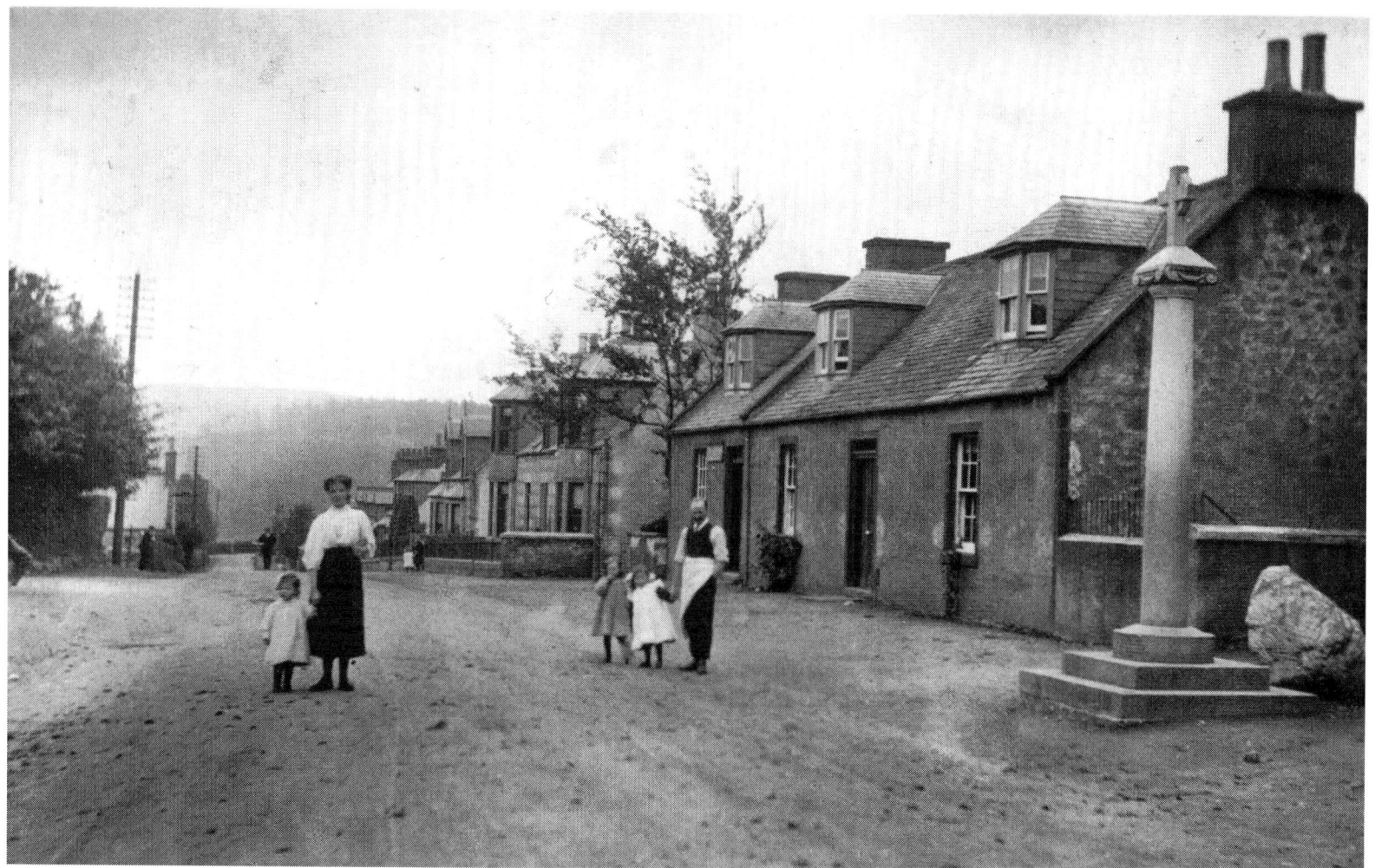

The Fastern's-een Cross was erected on the site of one of the chartered markets in the Royal Burgh of Fyvie to commemorate the coronation of Edward VII 1902. The Buchan Stone, a large white quartz stone marks the boundary between the districts of Buchan to the north and Formartine to the south. Both have since been relocated to the bus turning circle, situated beyond the school, on Cuminestown Road. The Mains of Fyvie Farm occupied this area until the mid-1800s as seen on early maps of Fyvie. The houses on the right became the offices for Alexander's buses and their garage depot was built at the rear. The premises were converted to a furniture showroom and workshop in 2004 by Neil Taylor.

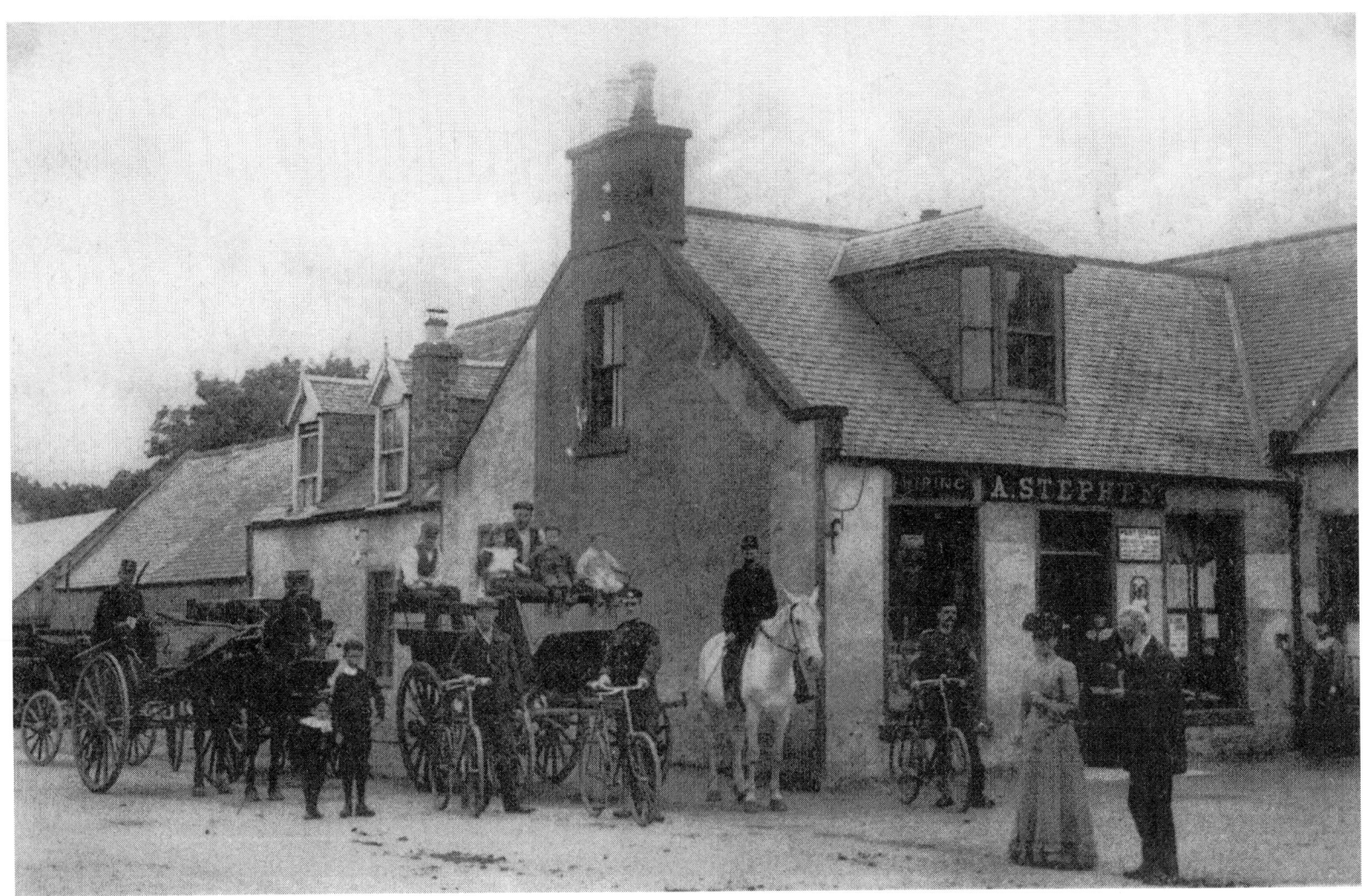

In Worral's directory of 1877 Alexander Stephen was the Fyvie postmaster. Post arrived from the north at 7.30 in the morning and was dispatched south at 8.15. Twice a day post would arrive from the south for distribution and its journey onward. In the early 1900's William Giles carried on and expanded the business. As well as selling grocery, drapery and haberdashery goods, Giles had floats, van deliveries, a farm and sold poultry to the London market. Plucking the turkeys at Christmas was a good earner for local children.

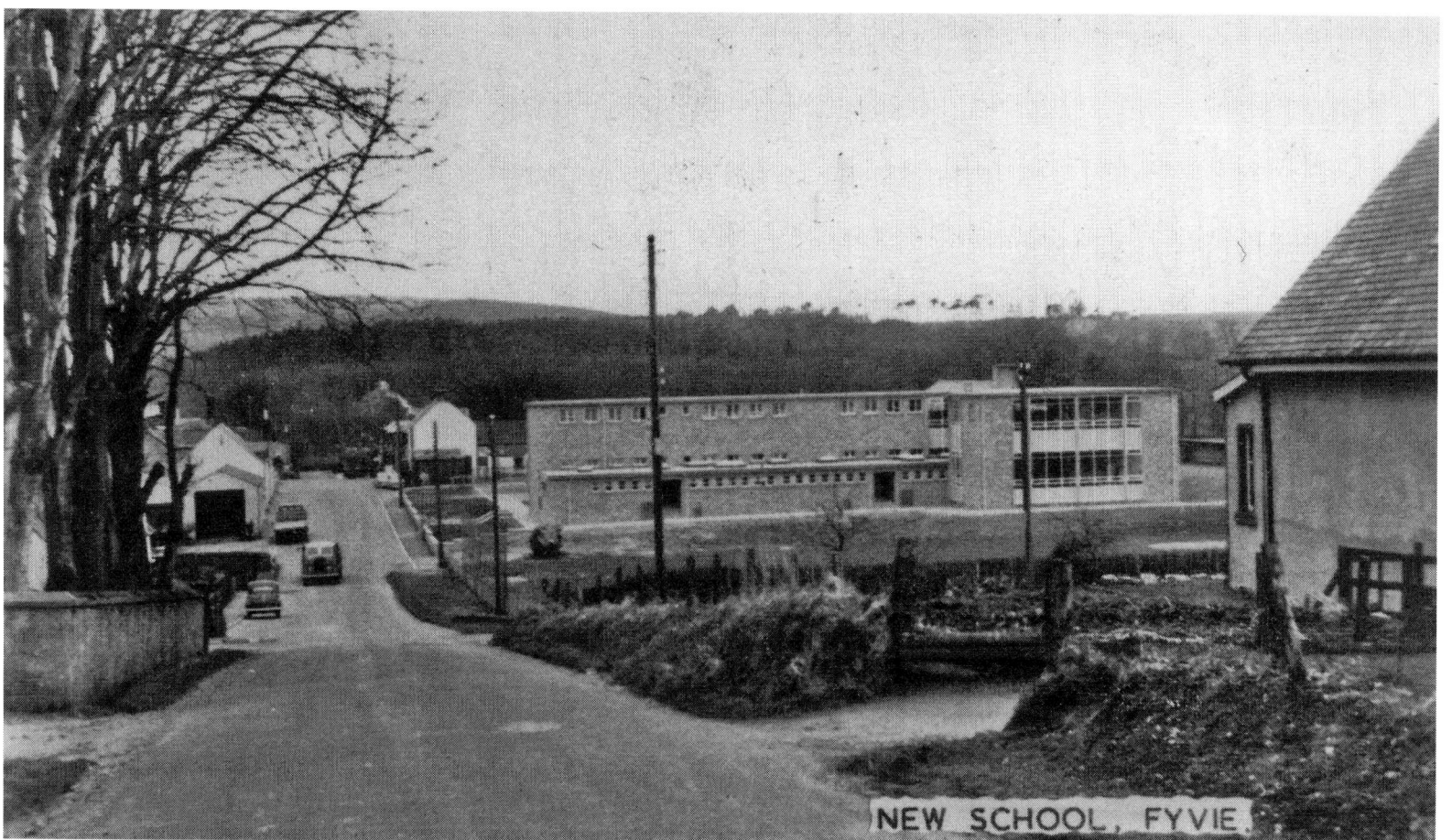

NEW SCHOOL, FYVIE

The first parts of the 'new' school were opened in May 1955 and are hidden behind this later extension to them. Twenty years had passed since the old school had been slated by the Scottish Education Department for its lack of facilities, with no assembly hall or gymnasium and limited class space for its pupils. It had been added to on several occasions but 'the continued increase in the number of pupils, necessitating ordinary class-work being carried out on in the school hall and in staff rooms together with the approach of the new Education Act, has compelled the Education Committeee to face the question of finding new accommodation'. Faced with the necessity of spending money Aberdeen County Council declined, claiming that the Department was acting in a 'somewhat high-handed' manner. Perhaps, they conceeded, there should be a new facility in the village for higher grade pupils, leaving the old school for infants and juniors, the opinion of the Department would be sought at a conference in Edinburgh. Whatever the outcome of those discussions the children of Fyvie had a long wait for a new school.

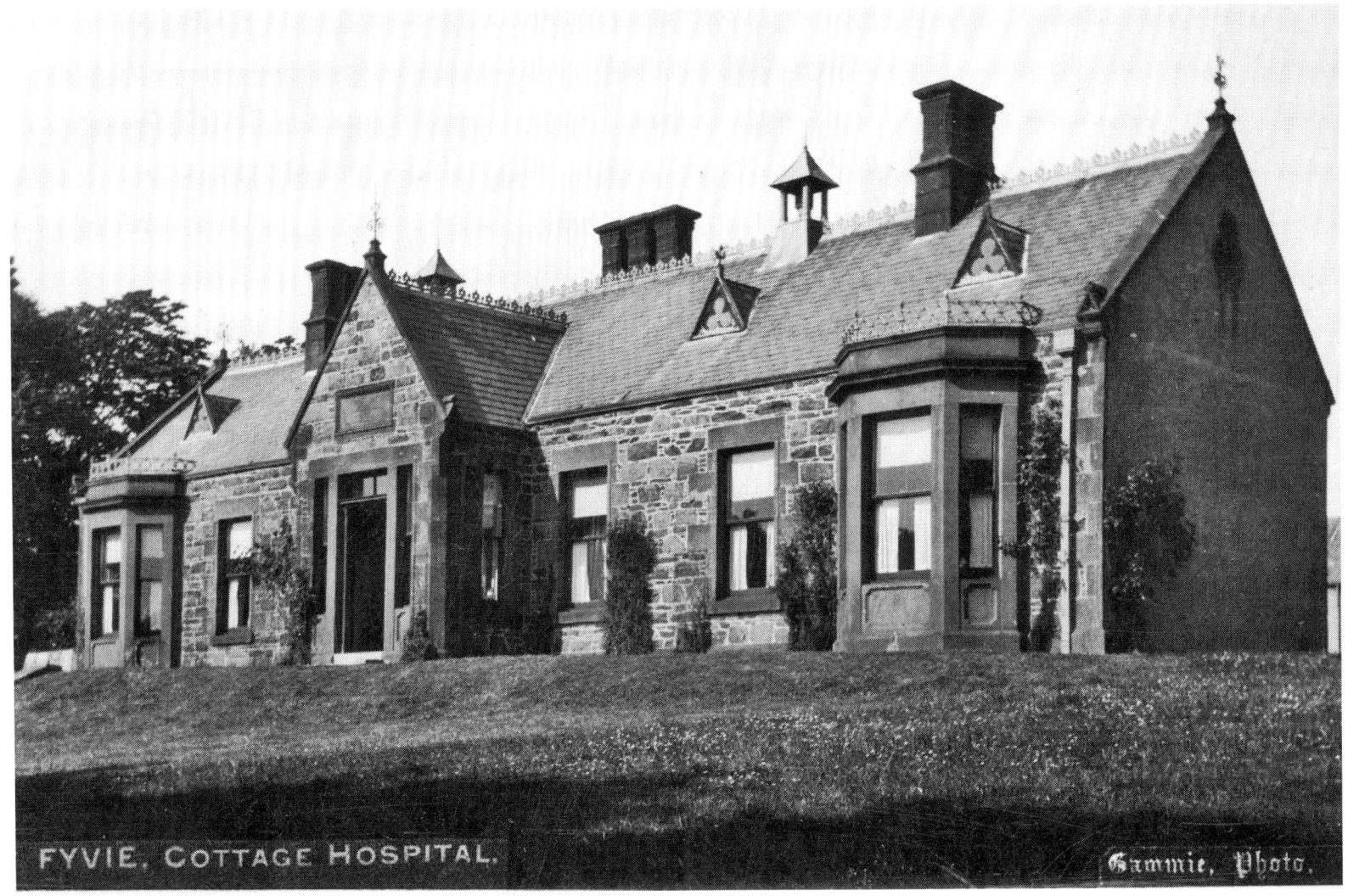

Fyvie Hospital was built by Colonel and Mrs Gordon of Fyvie in 1879. Designed by James Duncan, it housed seven beds intended for medical cases and surgical procedures. In 1907 Aberdeen County Council extended the building by adding two huts, to be used for cases of tuberculosis. It operated as an NHS maternity hospital until 1964 when it closed. Now owned by Aberdeenshire Guides it is used by Brownies for pack holidays.

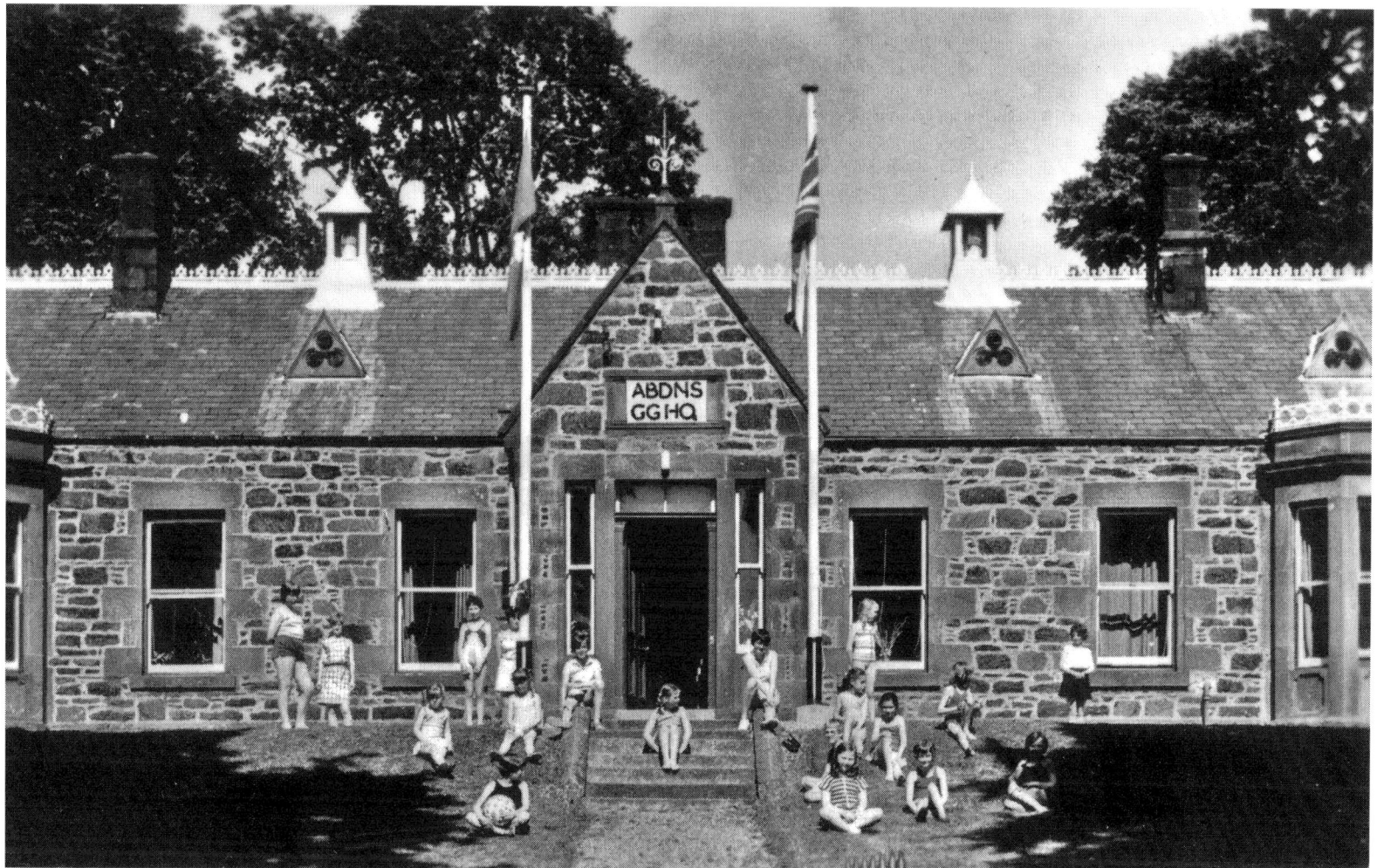

It was Alison Catto commisioner of Aberdeen Girl Guides, who spotted the potential of the former hospital. The Guides negotiated to buy the former hospital from Sir Ian Forbes Leith for £2,000 and acquired the building in November 1965, after a drive to raise money for its purchase, including a bazaar in Aberdeen Music Hall that raised £1,000. Then in April the following year, once red tape and small difficulties had been resolved they took posession. Work began to convert the old hospital to provide conference space, change the wards to dormitories for pack holidays, and training course space for the 2,500 strong Aberdeenshire Guides. It is still a valuable facility for Guide, Brownie and Rainbow groups across Aberdeenshire.

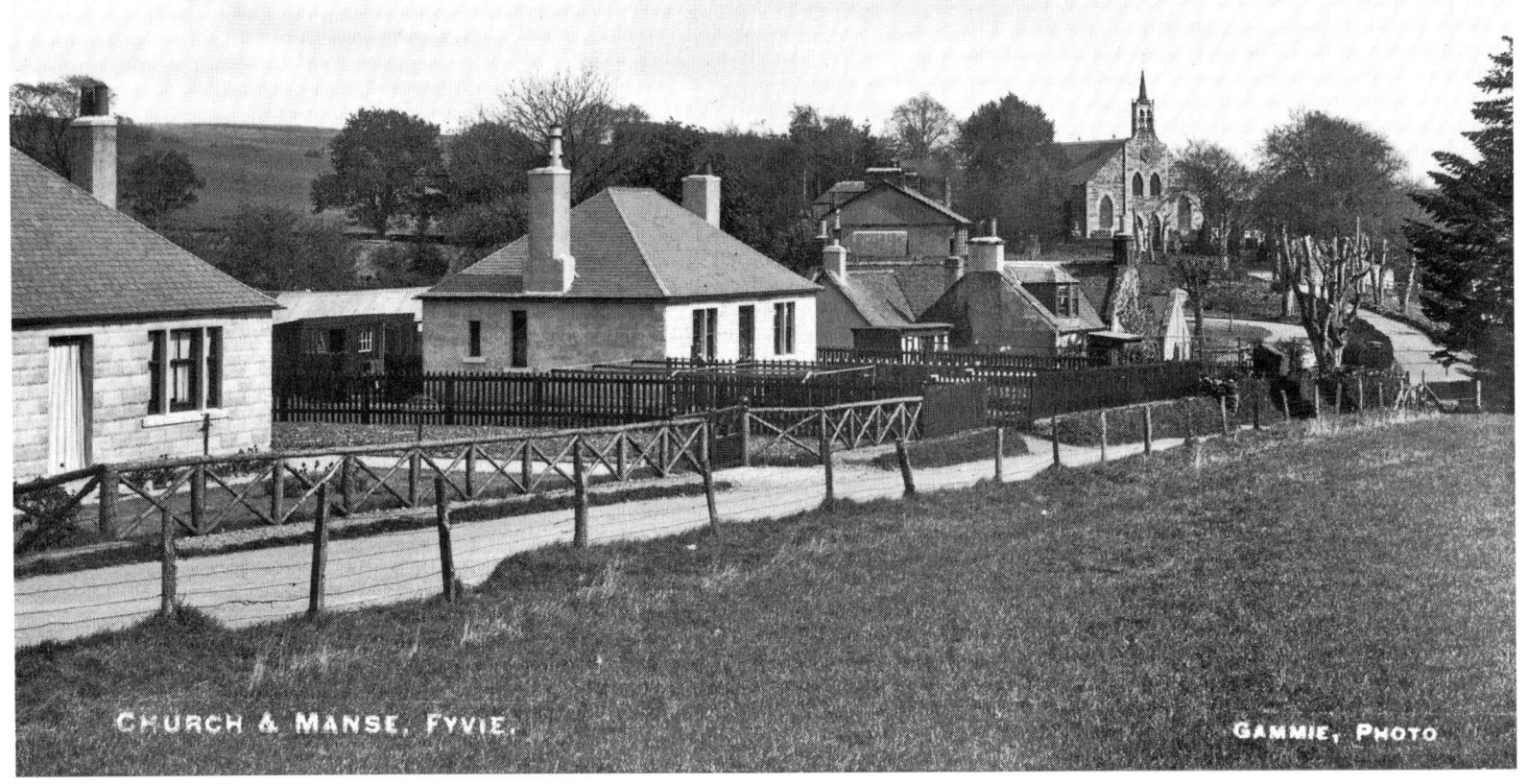

CHURCH & MANSE, FYVIE. GAMMIE, PHOTO

Private houses built by local builder A.B. Ogston in the 1930s on School Road include Pitmansy; Fae-me-well; Camiers; The Bungalow; Dinnyduff and Morven. The architects were Duncan & Munro and James Duncan's son William. The plans and drawings of the Duncans have been preserved and are kept in the Aberdeenshire archives.

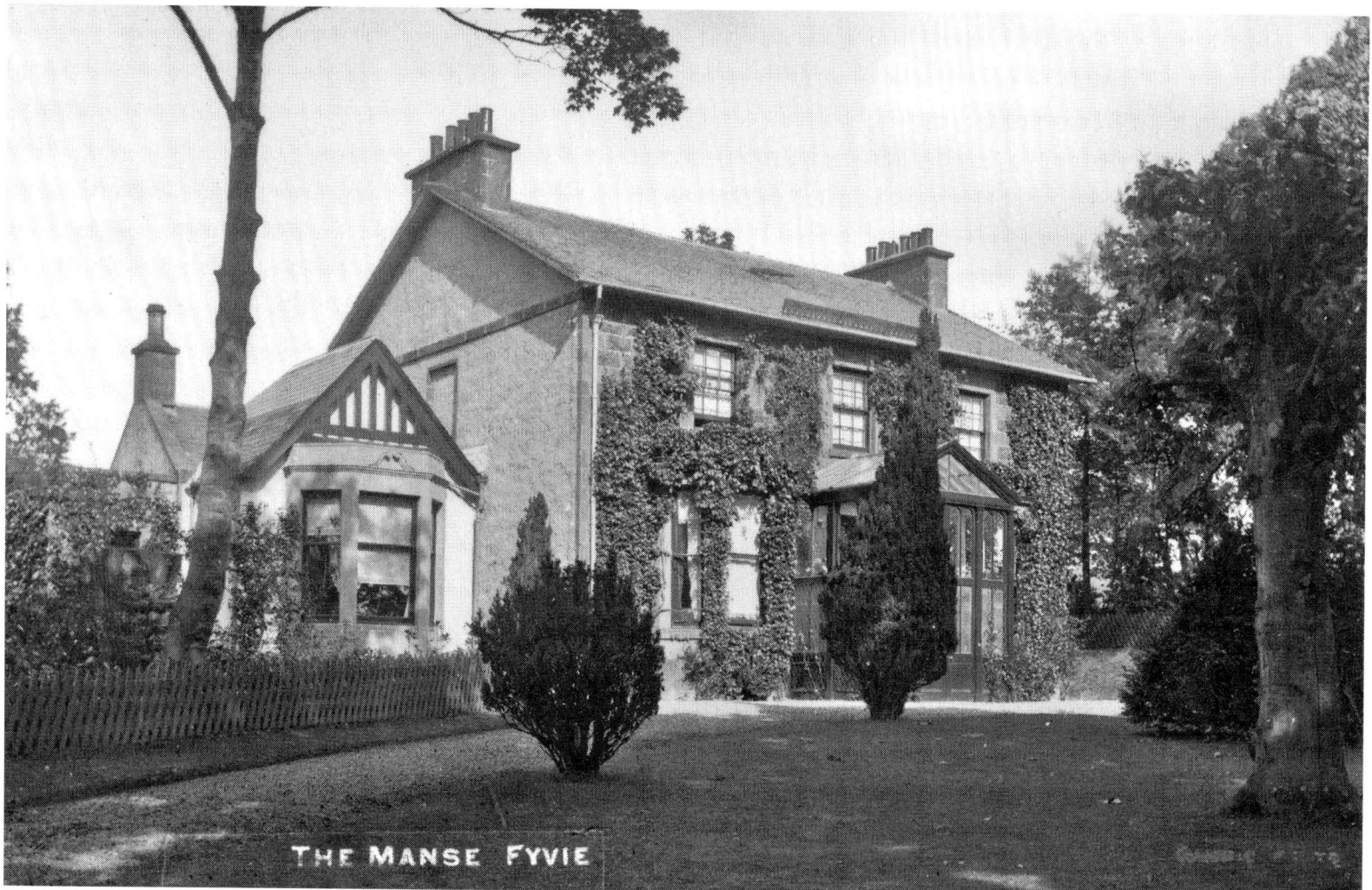

The Manse, Fyvie was built in 1830 to replace an earlier manse. Its construction was prompted by the death of the minister, Rev John Falconer in December 1828. The following year the furniture from the old manse was sold and the site cleared for the construction of this building. In 1831 the manse offices were added. It was the home of the ministers of Fyvie Church until a new manse was built in part of the manse garden. The old manse is now called Ardlogie House.

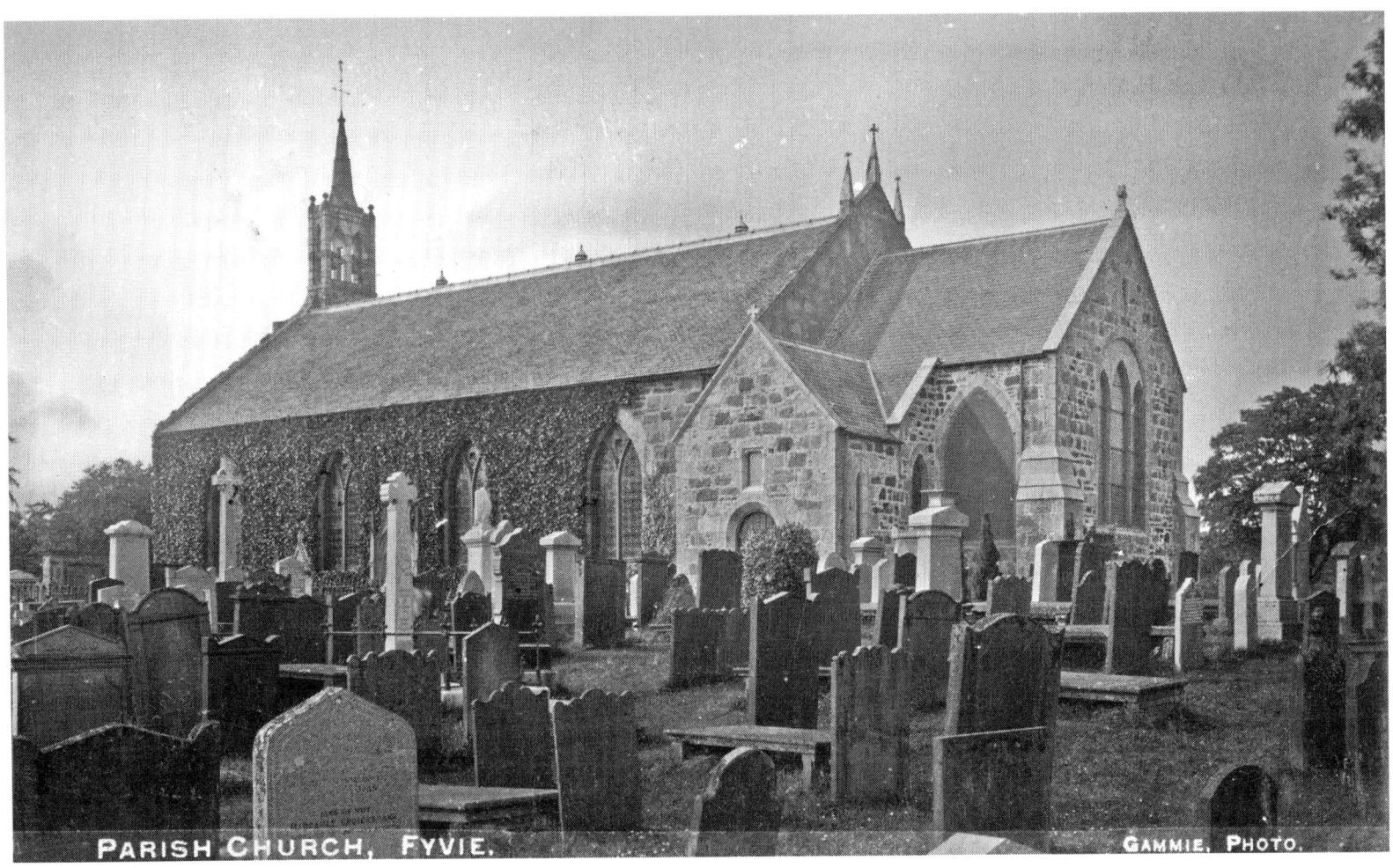

PARISH CHURCH, FYVIE. GAMMIE, PHOTO.

During the 12th century the Parish Church of Fyvie, was dedicated to St Peter. The present-day church was erected in 1808 and is thought to be the fourth to stand on or around this location. In 1904, the church was extended by the Forbes-Leith family to incorporate the stained-glass window, which commemorates their nineteen-year-old son Percy, who died of fever in the Boer War, 1900. The Laird's pew was added at the same time. In 1959 the Fyvie congregation was united with Woodhead Church, previously the Free Kirk. A further union occurred in 1974 with Millbrex and a link later followed with Rothienorman in 1993. Fyvie Church belongs to the Presbytery of Turriff.

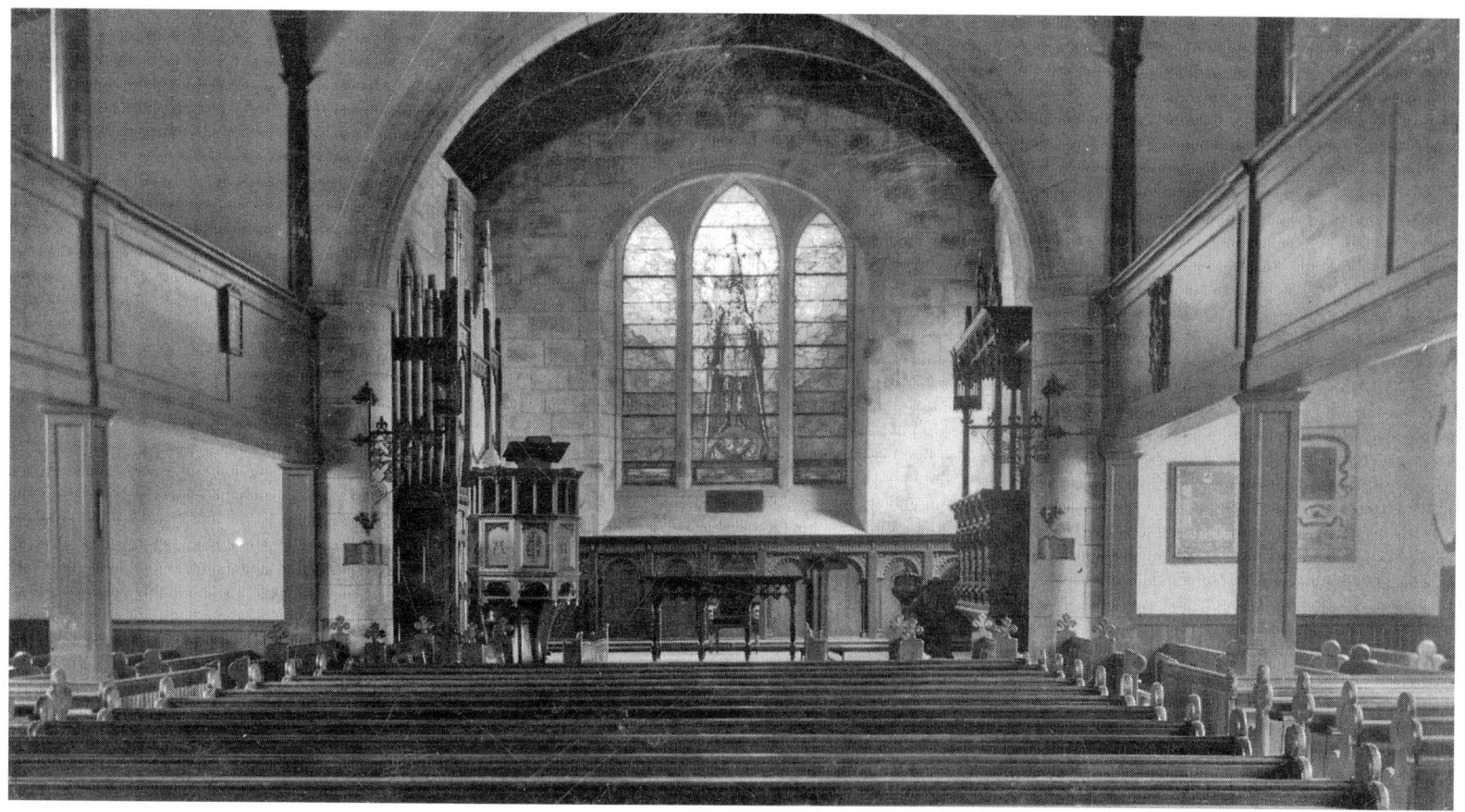

The chancel with a combined laird's aisle and organ chamber was built by the local Forbes Leith family, primarily to install the large Tiffany memorial window. The window was designed by Louis Comfort Tiffany, of Tiffany & Co. New York, one of two Tiffany windows in Scotland the other smaller example is in St. Cuthbert's Church, Edinburgh. The chancel is shorter and narrower than the nave and has a large round-arched window with plate tracery and three lancet openings in the east gable. Under the window on the east wall are set four carved stones in a rough cruciform shape. There are three Pictish symbol stones and a cross shaft. One stone shows part of an eagle while another depicts an elephant. High in the gable head is another reused stone, likely a finial from the medieval Priory in Fyvie. The focus of the chancel is the unique stained-glass window, a memorial to Percy Forbes-Leith. It is by Tiffany of New York and was a prototype design with unusual coloured and textured glass which varies in thickness. The stained glass window in the apse of Fyvie Church was gifted by American friends of the Forbes-Leith family, Lairds of Fyvie, in memory of Percy Forbes Forbes-Leith of the 1st Royal Dragoons who died of fever in 1900 whilst serving in South Africa. This exquisite work of art was created by Louis Comfort Tiffany, in his unique style and colouring, and depicts the Archangel St. Michael astride the Wheel of Time and bearing a flaming sword and the Banner of the Cross.

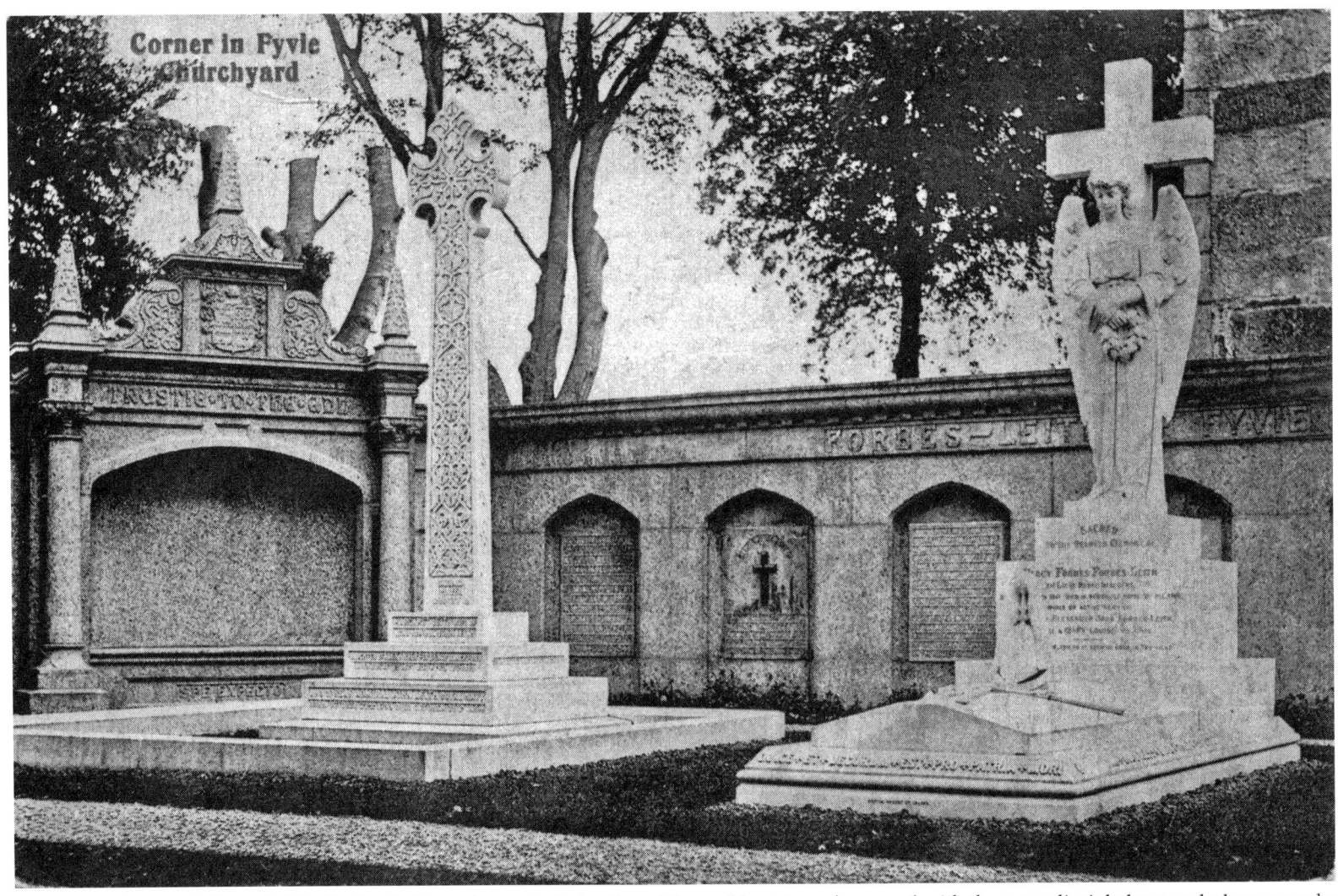

Laird's Family Burial Ground. The Forbes-Leith enclosure includes the white marble statue of an angel with the grenadier's helmet and plumes marks the grave of Percy Forbes-Leith to whom the Tiffany window is dedicated.

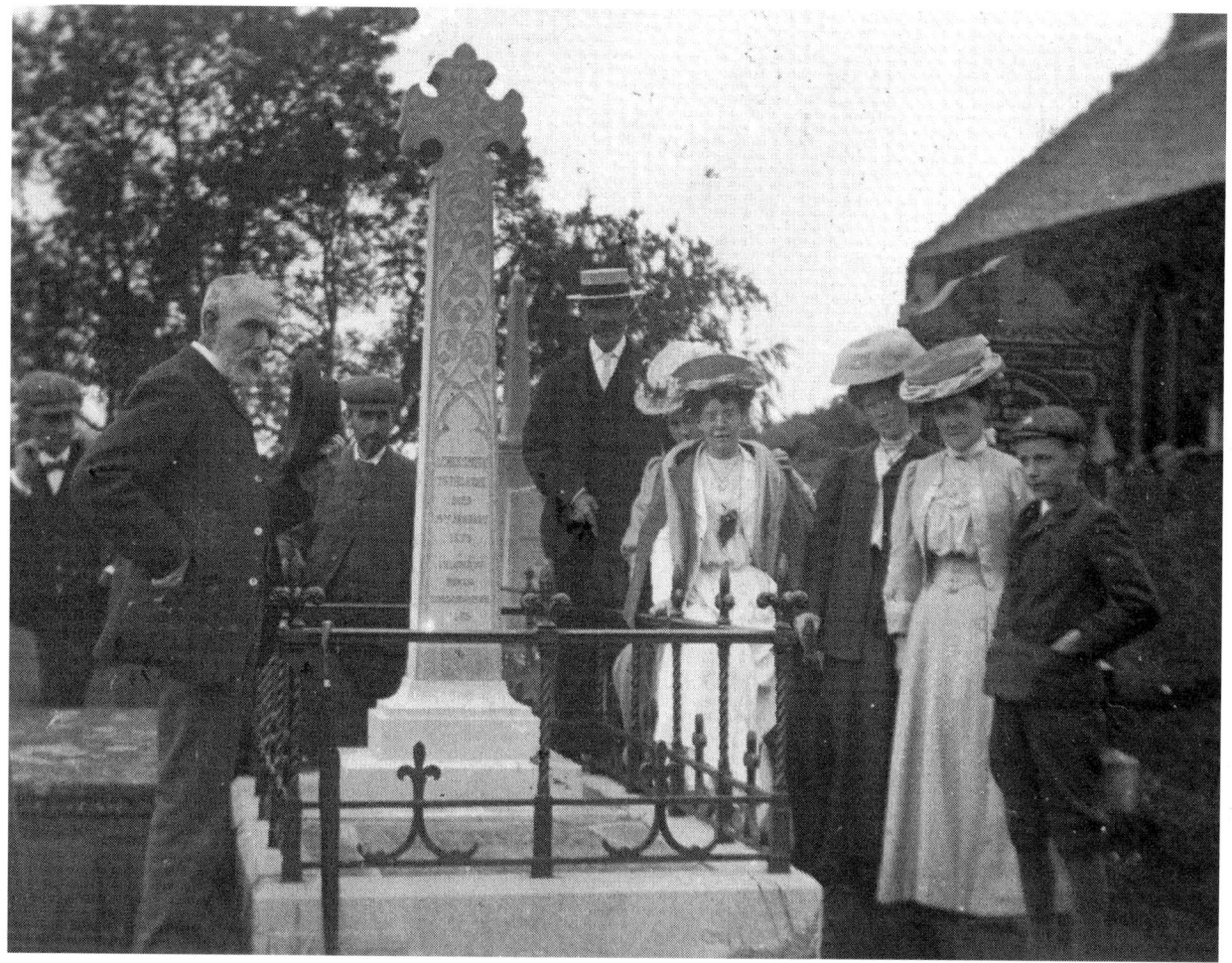

In the 17th century a ballad circulated throughout Scotland telling the sorry tale of Agnes or Annie Smith, daughter of the local miller, William Smith of Tifty. Her passionate romance with the laird's trumpeter, Andrew Lammie, was met with overwhelming family resistance. Even the intervention of Lord Fyvie, himself taken with Annie's beauty, was to no avail. Suffering dreadfully at the hands of her own family she died in January 1673 whilst Andrew was away in Edinburgh. Tifty's Annie was buried in Fyvie Kirkyard, her original headstone perished, and her grave is now marked by a Maltese stone cross surrounded by railings. It was funded by the public in 1859. Andrew Lammie is remembered through a sandstone figure, which stands on top of Fyvie Castle, his trumpet pointing towards Tifty.

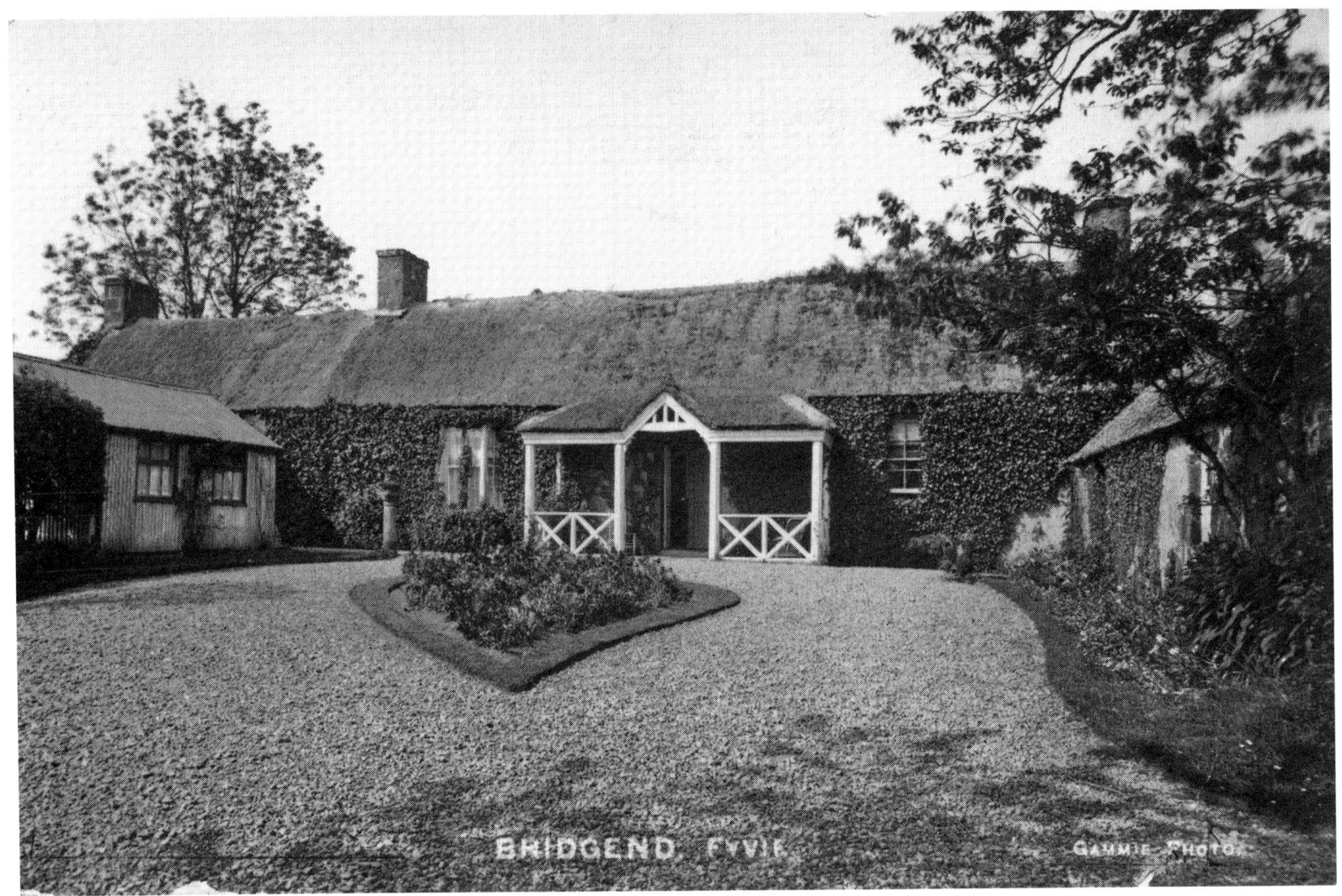

Bridgend was the home of Doctor Charles Greig. Fyvie was served by the Greig family for many years. Dr Alexander Greig M.R.C.S.E. Sunnyside, Fyvie for 42 years. He died in 1880. His son, Charles Cormack Greig M.B., C.M., continued as a medical practitioner in Fyvie for 54 years. He died in 1929. Plaques honouring and commemorating both doctors were erected by parishioners of Fyvie and can be seen on the south wall of Fyvie Church.

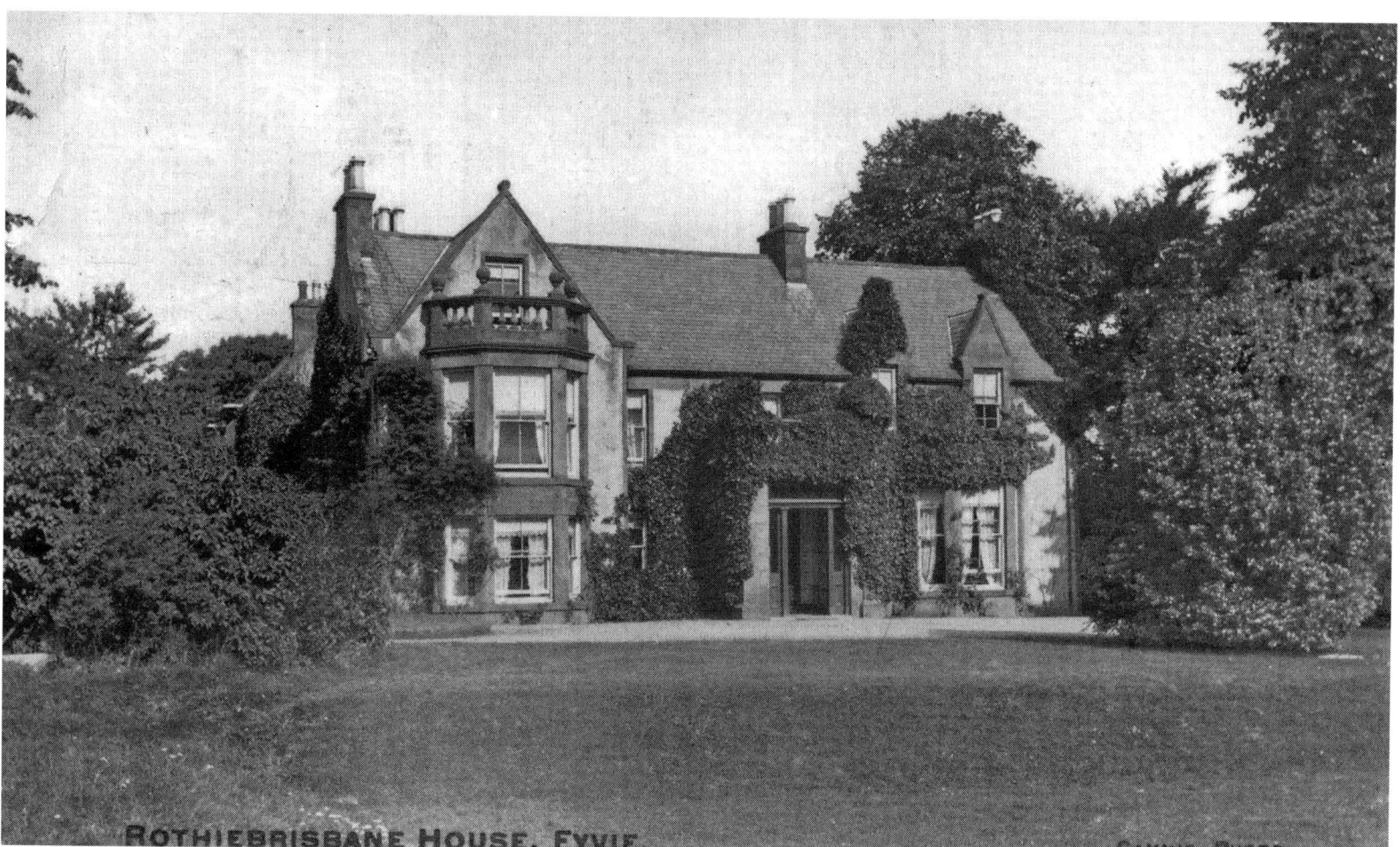

ROTHIEBRISBANE HOUSE, FYVIE.   GAMMIE, PHOTO.

About a mile west of Fyvie is Rothiebrisbane House. The lands of Rothiebrisbane, on Fyvie Estate, have been tenanted by three generations of the Ferguson family since 1935. The land was previously owned by the Chalmers family at Monkshill. In the 14th century the lands of Little Rothie were conferred by Robert the Bruce to two families, Norman and Brisbane, hence Rothienorman became the village and district and Rothiebrisbane the farm. In the 1800s the same Brisbane family gave their name to the city of Brisbane, Australia. In 1918 a special timber railway platform was erected at Rothiebrisbane Farm one mile south of Fyvie. The occasion was a shorthorn cattle sale and the excursion train had to pull forward more than once to allow passengers to disembark. The Rothiebrisbane Platform was only in use for five hours and five minutes. A temporary platform construction was not unusual, but a single use one, for such a short time was exceptional.

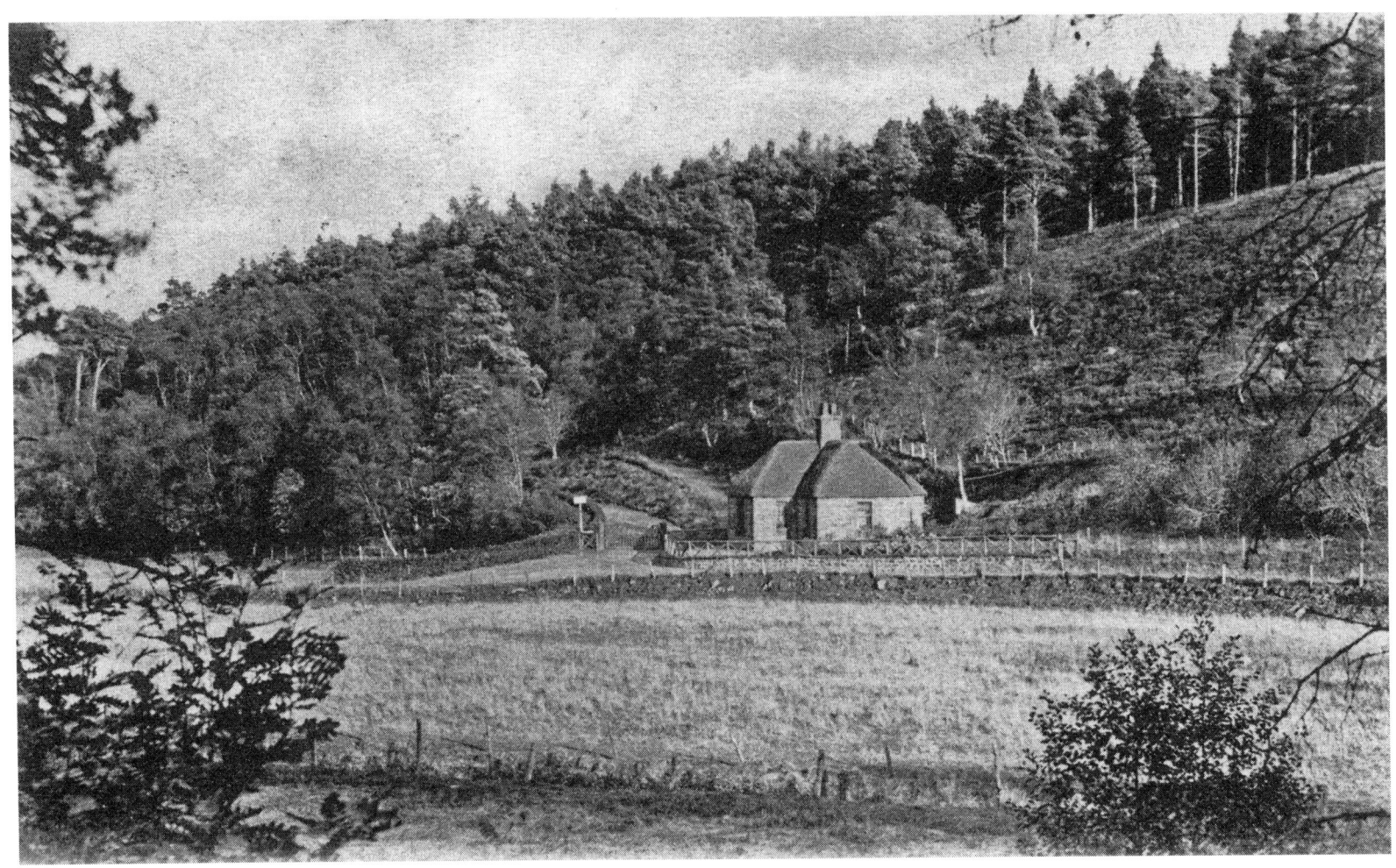

The south lodge of the Den of Rothie, near where the Fordoun Burn enters the wood before flowing through the narrow valley to Fordoun Bridge. Den is from the Old English *Denu* meaning a narrow valley or ravine. The usage has widened in Scots to include the woods that are often found in such features. The Den of Rothie is a plantation established by Colonel Gordon of Fyvie Castle. *The Present State of Husbandry in Scotland* (1784), notes the plantation '...was planted with fir about twelve years ago. No plantation is in a more vigorous state; and as it consists of 1000 acres will be of an immense value fifty years hence...'. Those words had come true by the time of the *New Statistical Account* (1845), where it states the wood '... produces considerable revenue.' Its true value now is as a haven for wildlife, and for the walks along its forest tracks.

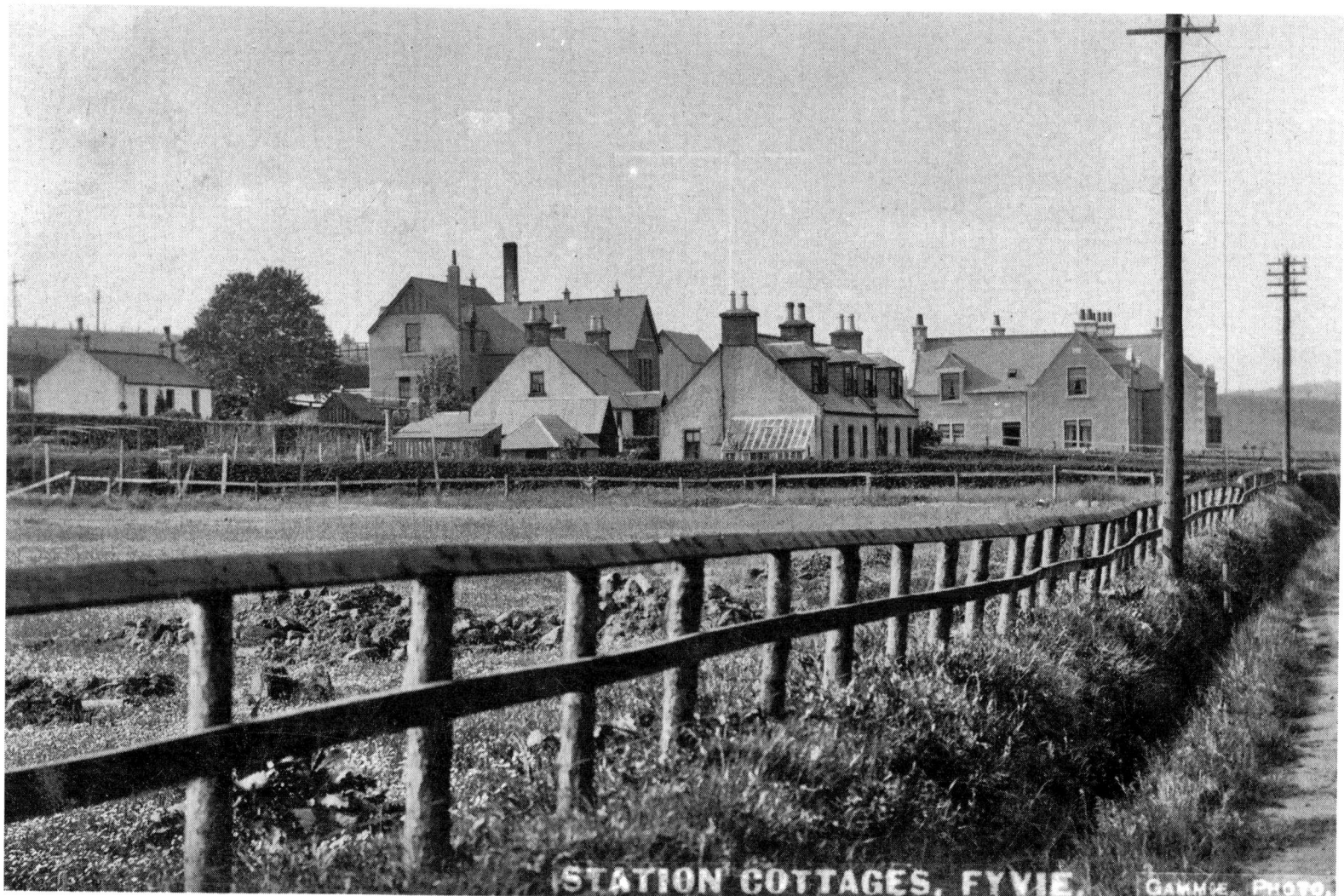

Built one mile north of the village the station was opened on 5th September 1857. The line went from Inveramsay near Inverurie, to Macduff on the north-east coast. It closed to passengers on 1st October 1951 and to goods on 3rd January 1966. In 1962 a special train took guests from Fyvie to Sir Andrew Forbes-Leith's wedding in Dumfries.

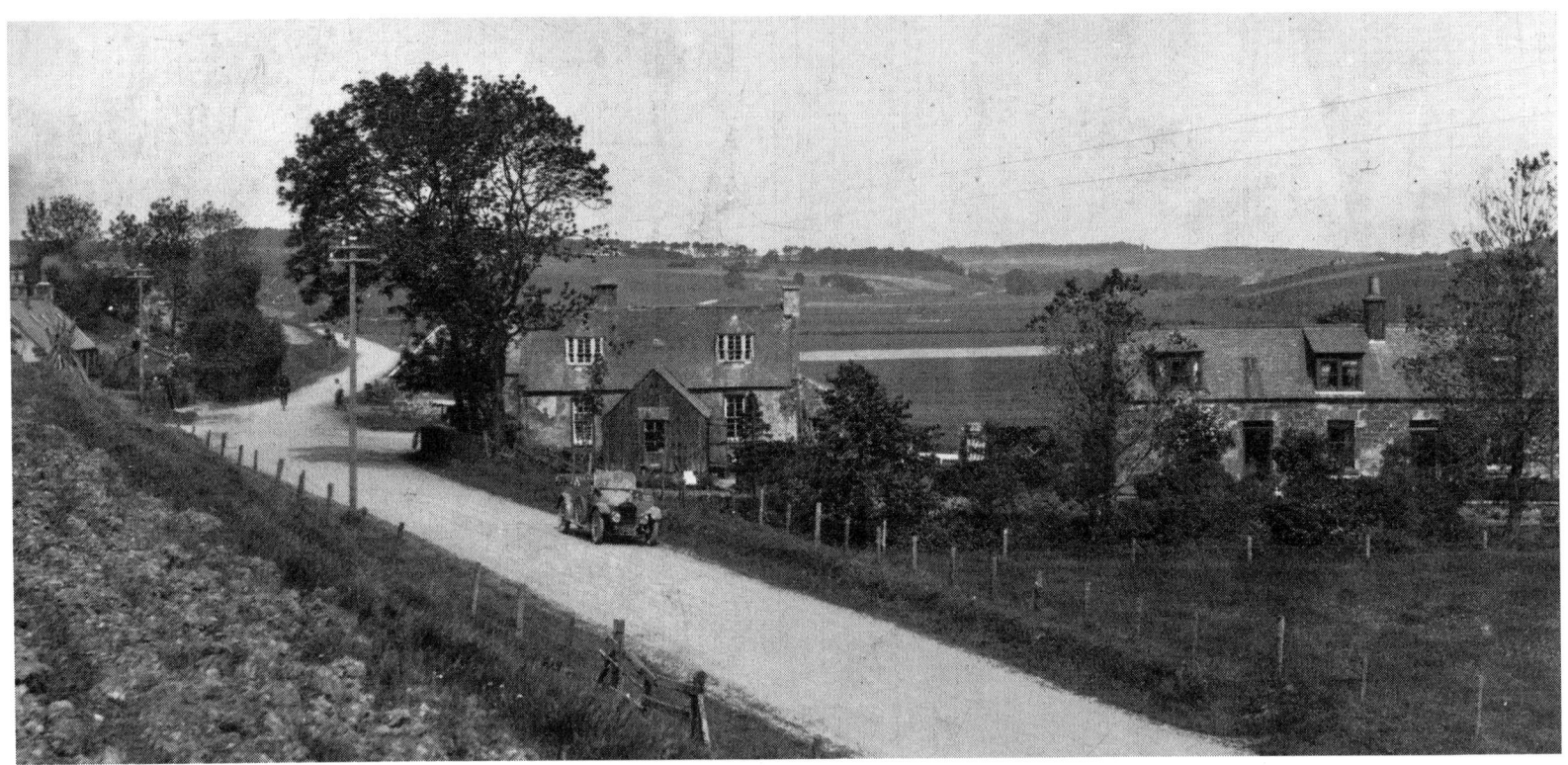

Inverythan is a small collection of houses just to the north of Fyvie Castle. At the time of the photograph in the 1930s there was still a shop and smithy. It is best known for the railway accident that happened on 27th November, 1882 at 4.57 pm. A mixed train of five goods wagons and four passenger carriages left Banff heading south to Aberdeen. Just south of Inverythan where the line crossed the turnpike road the bridge collapsed, killing eight people and injuring fourteen others. The bridge was formed from a pair of huge cast-iron beams with timbers between them, the beam which failed was found to have been poorly cast with numerous defects. The locomotive made it safely across the bridge, but as it reached the other side the coupling with the tender parted, and relieved of the weight of its train the engine shot forward. Two of the goods wagons and the tender came off the rails and tumbled down the railway embankment. The remaining three goods wagons and two third class carriages crashed through the bridge and were reduced to matchwood on the road below. The two following coaches remained on the railway above, the first class carriage suspended, resting on the debris below. A rescue train was quickly organised in Aberdeen and arrived at Fyvie at 8.35 pm, joining the local people who were already tending to the injured and clearing debris. A happier ending occured on Friday 29th December 1945, in another railway accident at Inverythan when a train derailed, this time on the bridge over the River Ythan. Fortunately the train remained on the tracks and none of the 30 passengers were hurt. Their ordeal wasn't over, in order to reach safety they had to walk along the 15 inch wide parapet of the bridge over the river which was in full spate. Helping the children and elderly passengers down from the embankment, they then walked to the road and flagged down a service bus, that by luck was passing. With everyone aboard they were able to continue their journeys, apparently with little delay!

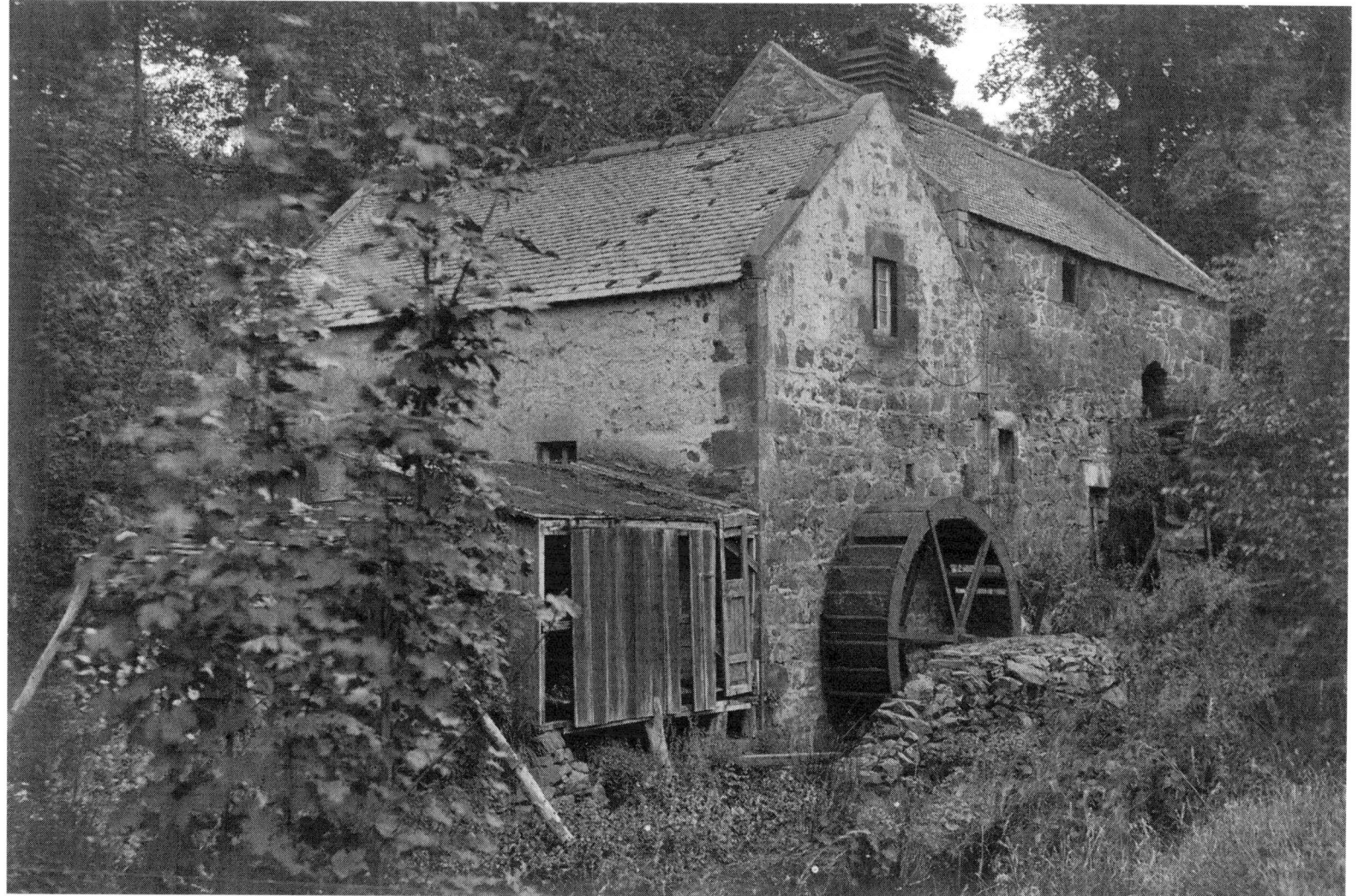

The Mill of Tifty was one of seven mills in the Fyvie area: Mill of Milton, Mill of Crichie, Mill of Ardlogie, Mill of Petty, Mill of Rothiebrisbane, Mill of Burns. They were powered by water and used for grinding corn grain to make oatmeal which was a staple part of the diet at the time. Oatmeal was used for brose, porridge, oatcakes and stuffing.

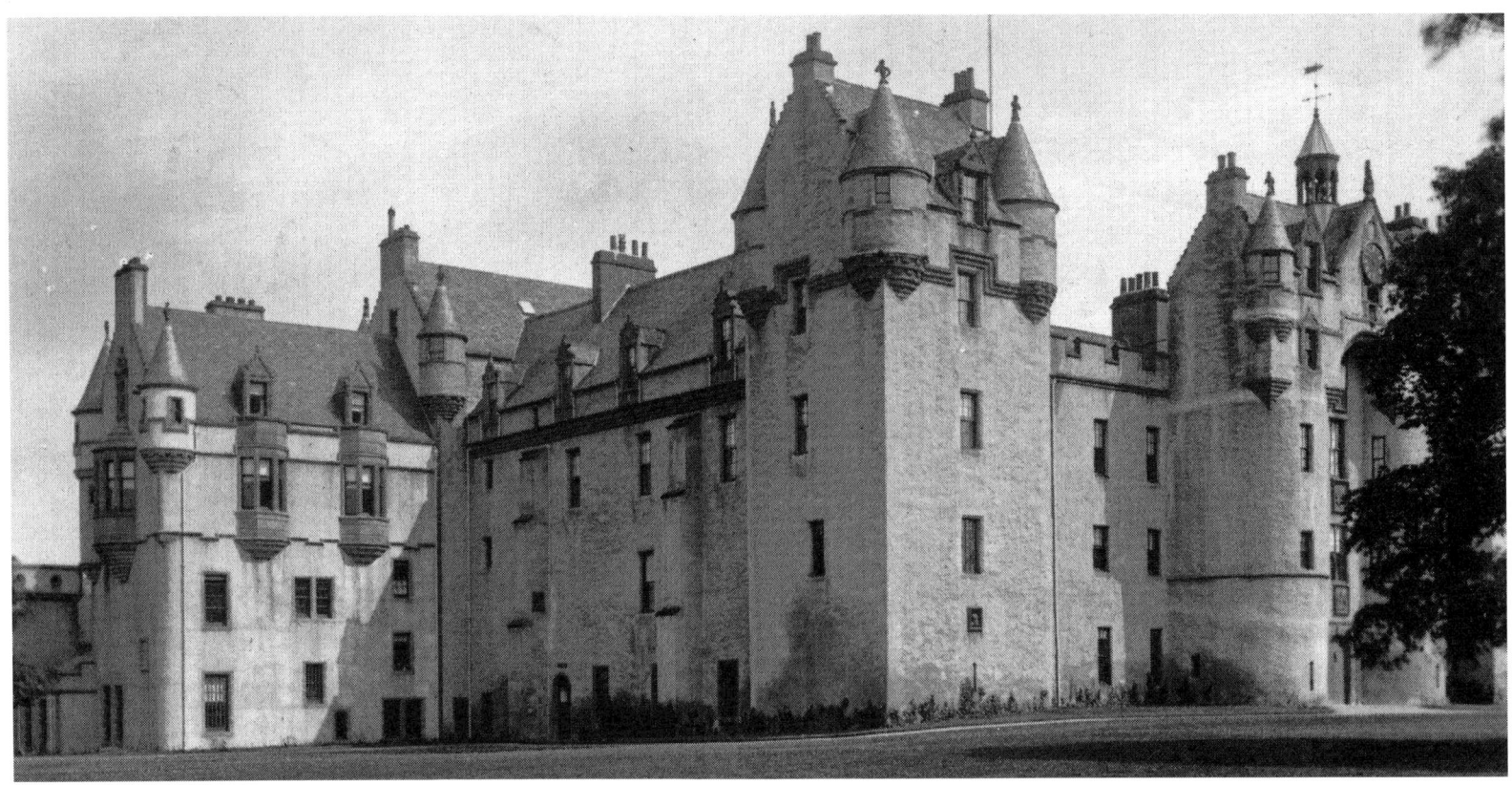

The earliest parts of Fyvie Castle date to the 13th century. It was a Royal Castle until 1370 when Robert II granted it to his son the Earl of Carrick, then passing through the Lyndsay, Preston, Meldrum and Seton families who each owned the castle for a while. It was seized by the Crown after the Seton family's involvement in the Jacobite rising of 1689. William Gordon 2nd Earl of Aberdeen bought it in 1733 from the Crown, and passed it to the eldest son from his third marriage, also William Gordon. He was nine when his father died in 1745, his career in Parliament and as a commisioned officer kept him away from Aberdeenshire. However, it was under his tenure that the castle was remodelled, the Gordon Tower built; the estate landscaped, including the construction of the ornamental loch, and the woods in the Den of Fyvie planted. The castle passed through several lines of the Gordon family until Sir Maurice Duff-Gordon was forced to sell it in 1885, it was bought four years later by Alexander John Forbes-Leith. He was a Scottish Royal Navy officer whose family came from Blackford near Fyvie. In 1871 he married American heiress Marie Louise January, left the Navy and moved to the USA. Forbes-Leith eventually became president of the Joliet Iron and Steel Company, and later director of United States Steel Corporation. With the money that he made in steel, in 1889 he bought Fyvie Castle in Aberdeenshire and in 1905 he was raised to the peerage as Baron Leith of Fyvie. The Leith Tower on the left was added by him. He died without a male heir. His daughter Ethel and her husband Charles Burn inherited the property. Today Fyvie Castle is owned by the National Trust for Scotland.

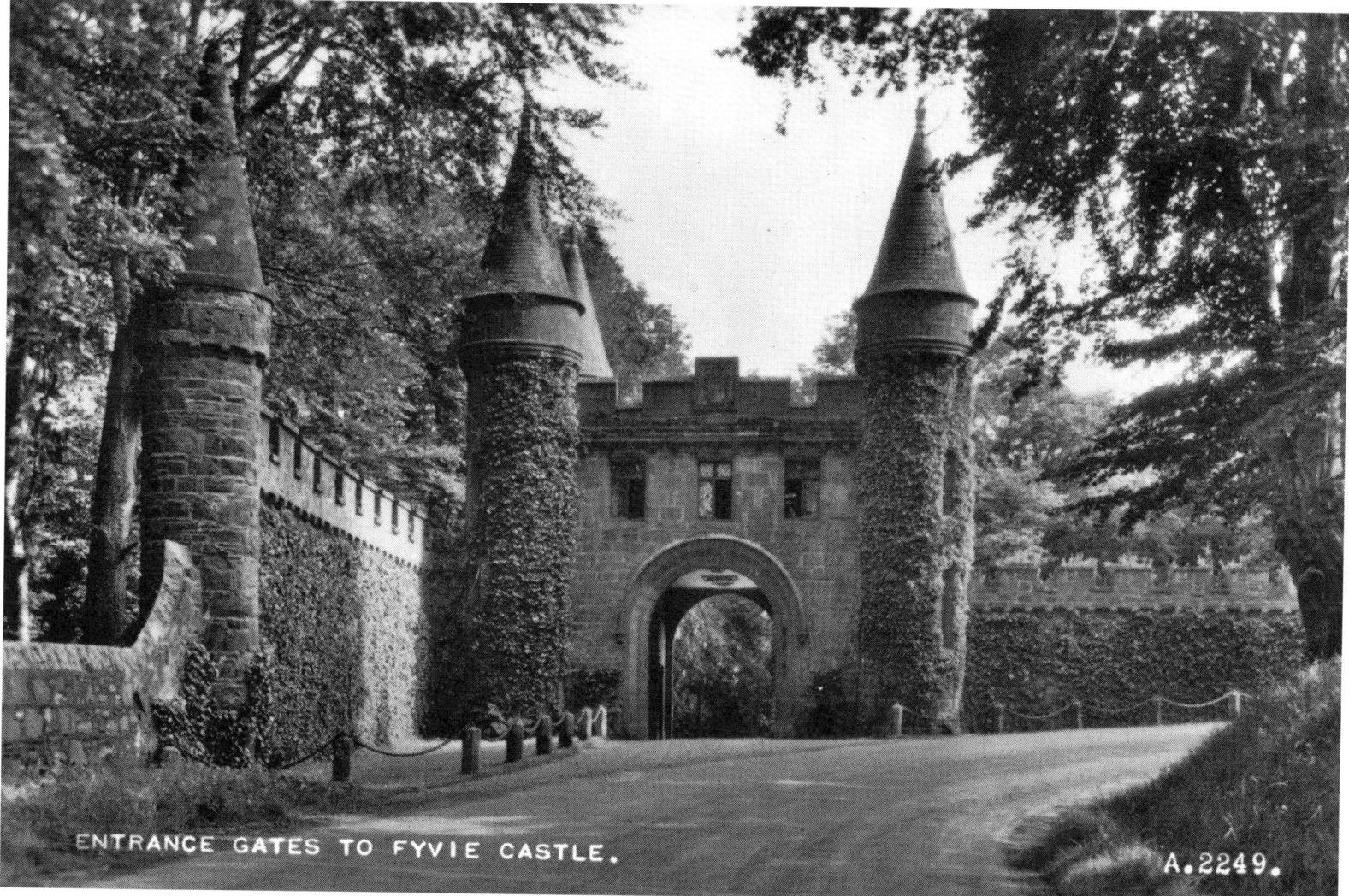

ENTRANCE GATES TO FYVIE CASTLE. A.2249.

North Lodge, dated 1819, also known as the chain lodge. It has a semi-circular arched pend with a 3-window lodge flat over it, circular angle towers corbelled out near top with conical roofs, corbelled and crenelated parapet. Crenelated screen walls run out at right angles to spired circular piers. Pinned rubble with red sandstone dressings. The main road used to run close past this lodge on the A947.

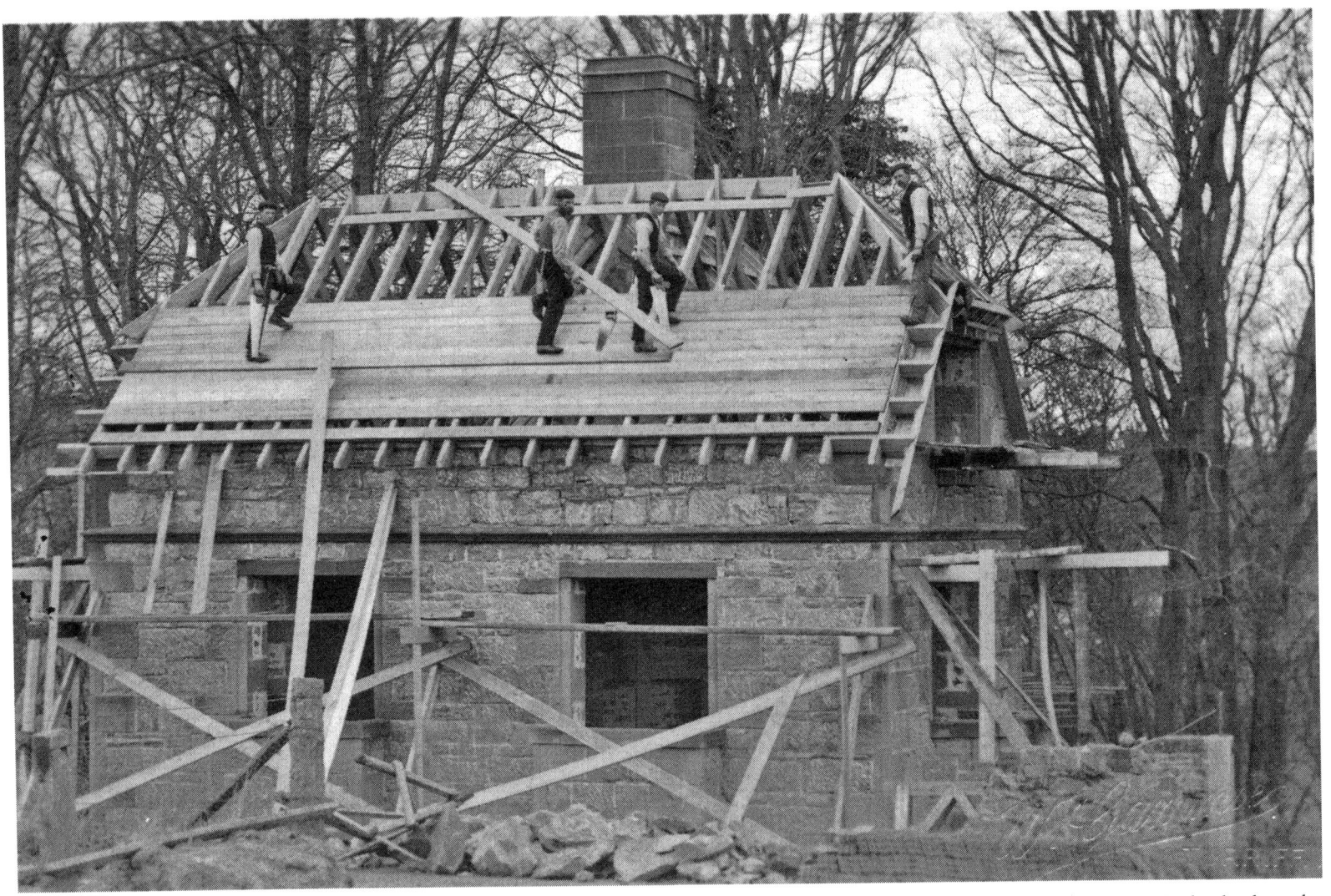

West Lodge. Built close to the road leading north from Fyvie at Fyvie Station. The date on the gate is 1906. The footpath from West Lodge leads to the castle via the Ivy Bridge across the River Ythan. In 2020 a lorry accident severely damaged the original gate, house and estate wall. The upstairs of the lodge formerly was used as an office by the laird's secretary.

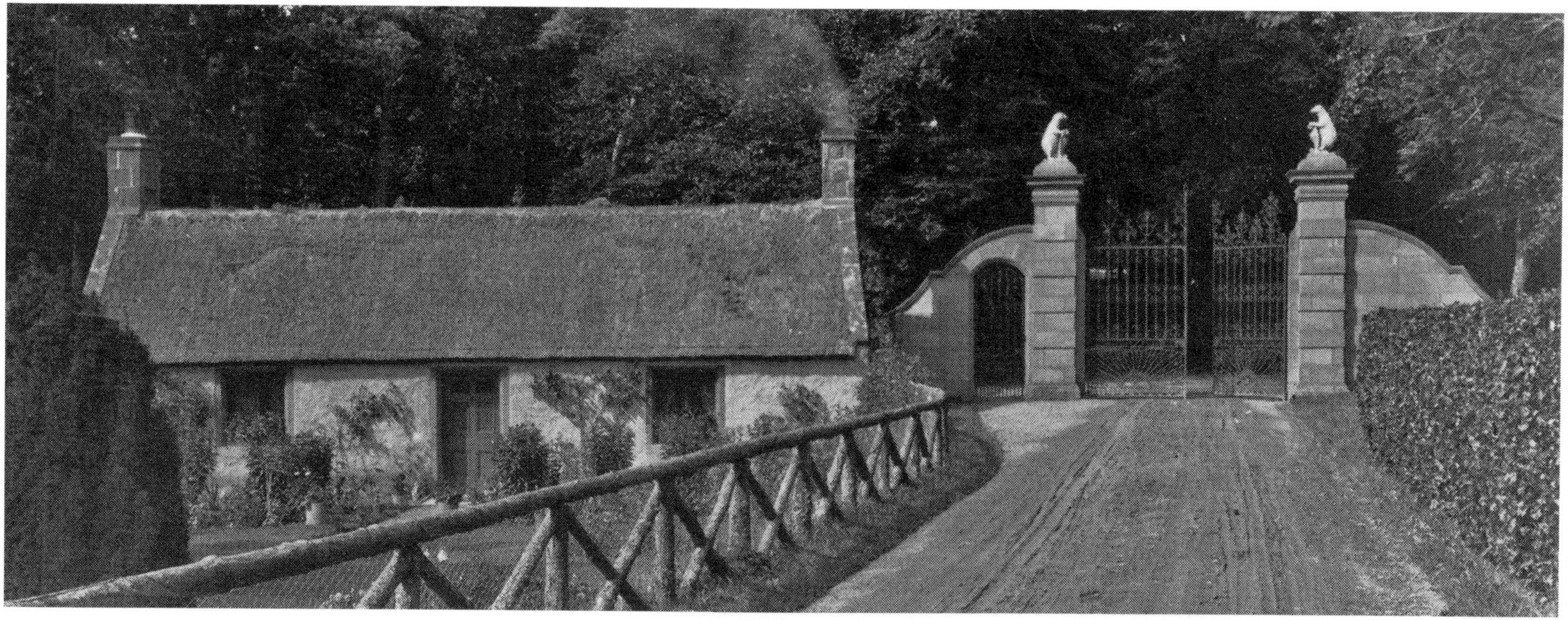

South Lodge. The entrance to the Castle policies is distinguished by John Bryce's south gates, (c.1890), comprising rusticated red ashlar piers, with flank walls, and intricate wrought iron gates. The gates were moved a few metres by the NTS in 1985 to make a new wider entrance to the road leading to the castle via the south side of the manmade lake. The road used to be private for the laird and his family only.

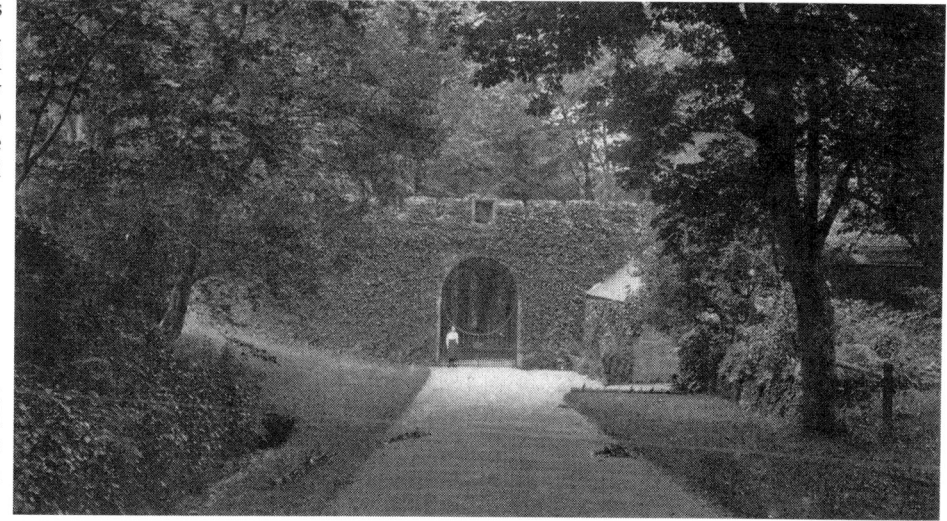

East Lodge. Built shortly after 1816, a screen wall cutting across the drive with a semi-circular parapet and a terminal circular pinnacle. Rubble in thin courses. The lodge house is a plain cottage with two windows and a central door with margins. All the lodges are listed buildings.

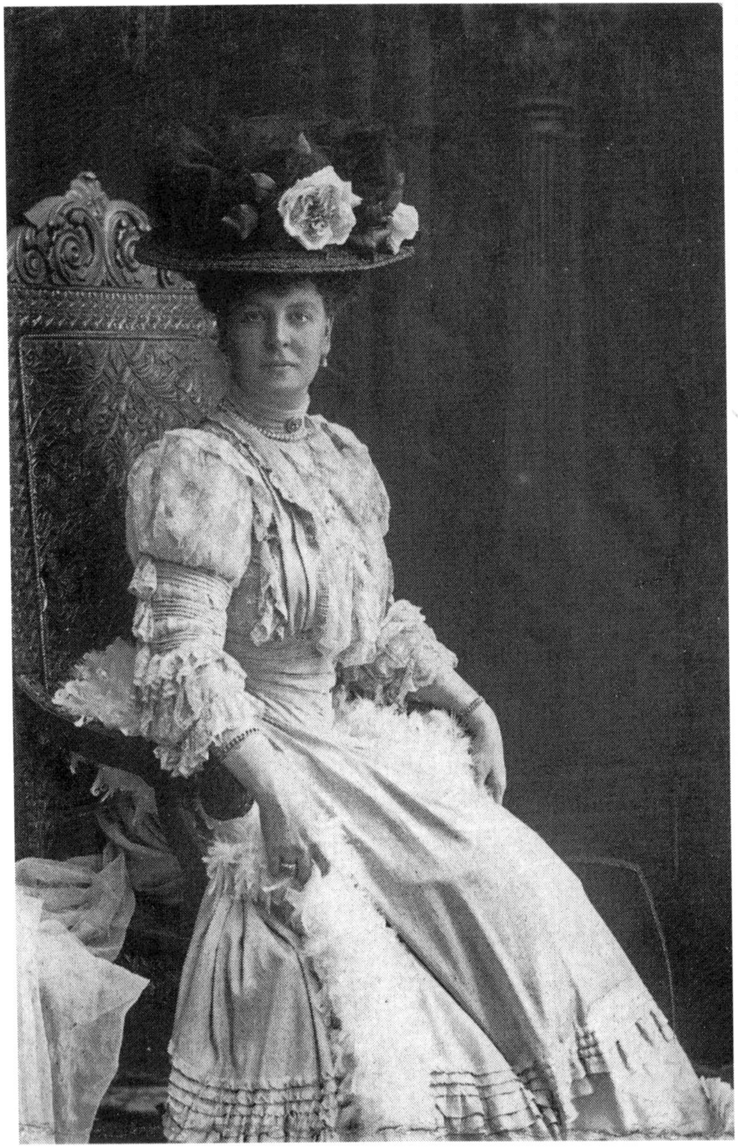

Ethel Forbes-Leith / Mrs Burns 1872-1930. Ethel Forbes'-Leith was the daughter of Alexander John Forbes-Leith, 1st and last Baron Leith of Fyvie, and American heiress Marie Louise January. She was Commandant and Matron at Stoodley Knowle Auxiliary Hospital, Torquay, during the First World War. Her son Arthur was killed in action in 1914. She was awarded the Order of St John of Jerusalem and the OBE. Her husband, Colonel Burn, took her surname when she inherited the Fyvie estates.

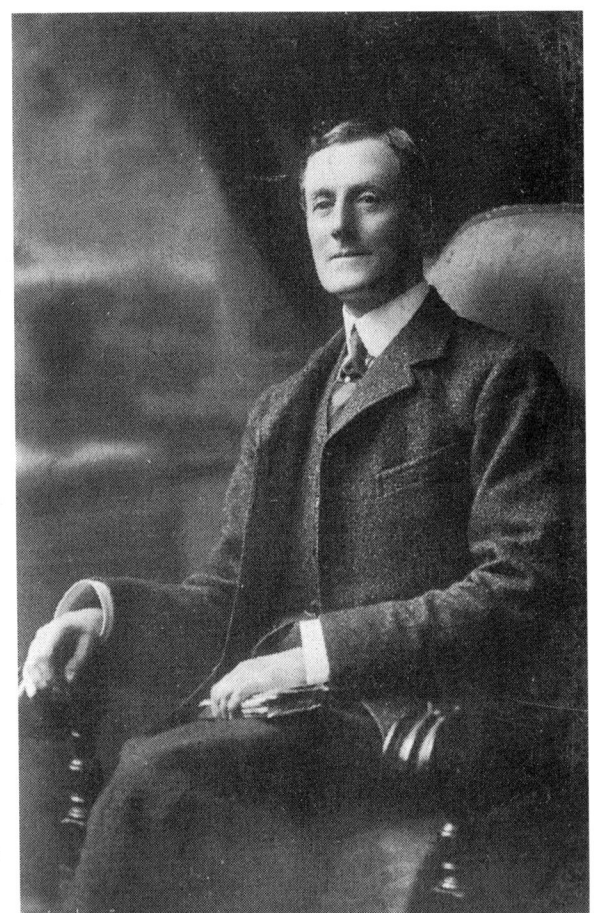

Col. Burns. Known as Charles Burn until 1923 and as Sir Charles Burn, Bt, between 1923 and 1925, he was a British army officer and Conservative Party politician. Aide-de-camp to H.M. The King. He had served in the 8th Hussars and the 1st Dragoons, before being transferred to the 3rd (Militia) Battalion of the Gordon Highlanders in 1899. He was seconded for service with the Imperial Yeomanry in South Africa on 31st January 1900, after the outbreak of the Second Boer War, and was in command of a Battalion. He later served with the Westminster Dragoons. Colonel Sir Charles Rosdew Forbes-Leith, 1st Baronet (1859-1930) was first elected as Torquay's Conservative MP in 1910 and served for the next 13 years.

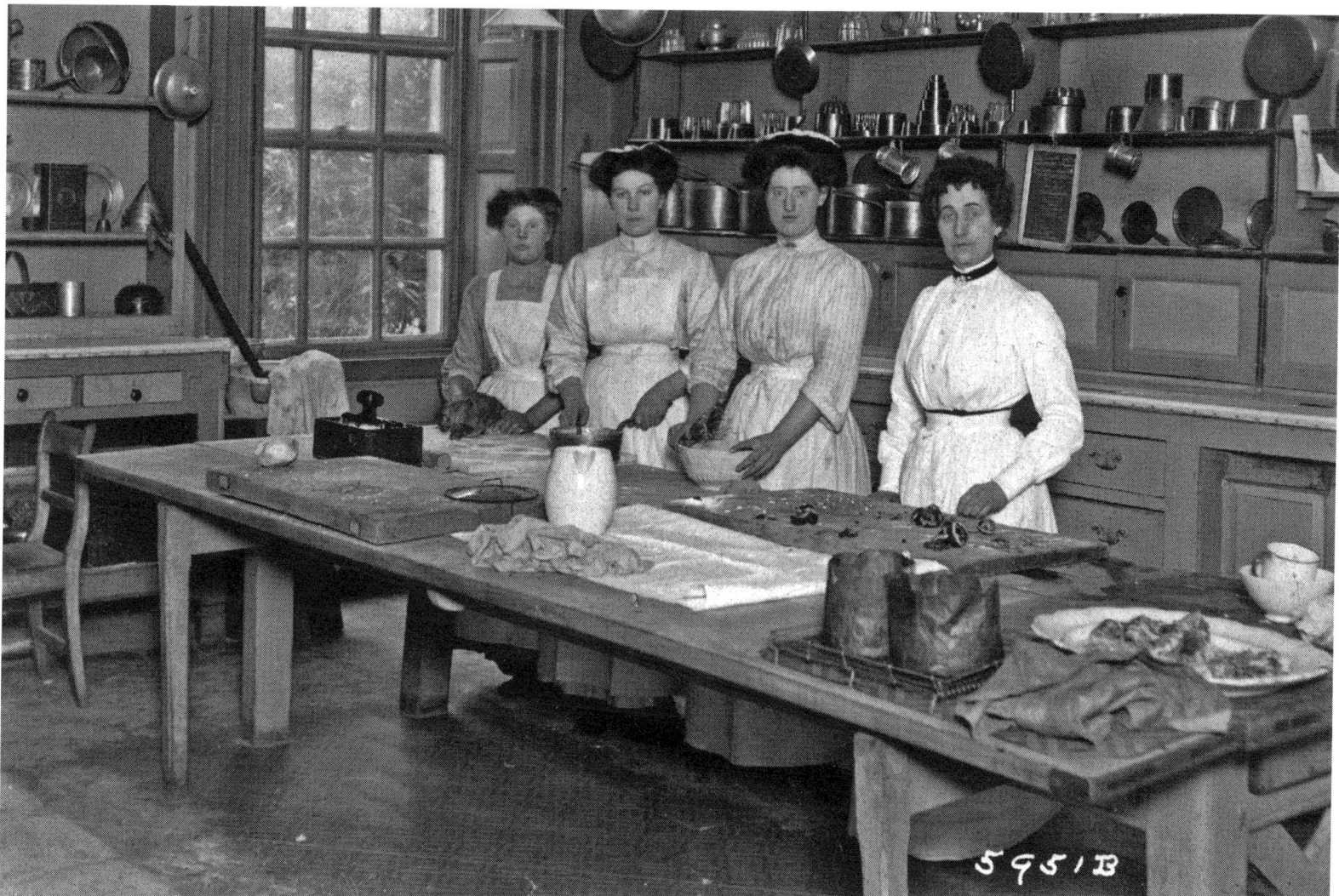

The kitchen at Fyvie Castle. The old kitchen is currently the tearoom for visitors to the National Trust of Scotland property at Fyvie. The kitchen range and all the old copper ware is on display there. A dumb waiter in the kitchen lifts the dishes of food up to the butler's pantry next to the dining room, far quicker and easier for the staff than taking the stairs. The castle also had an icehouse and cold larder for game etc.

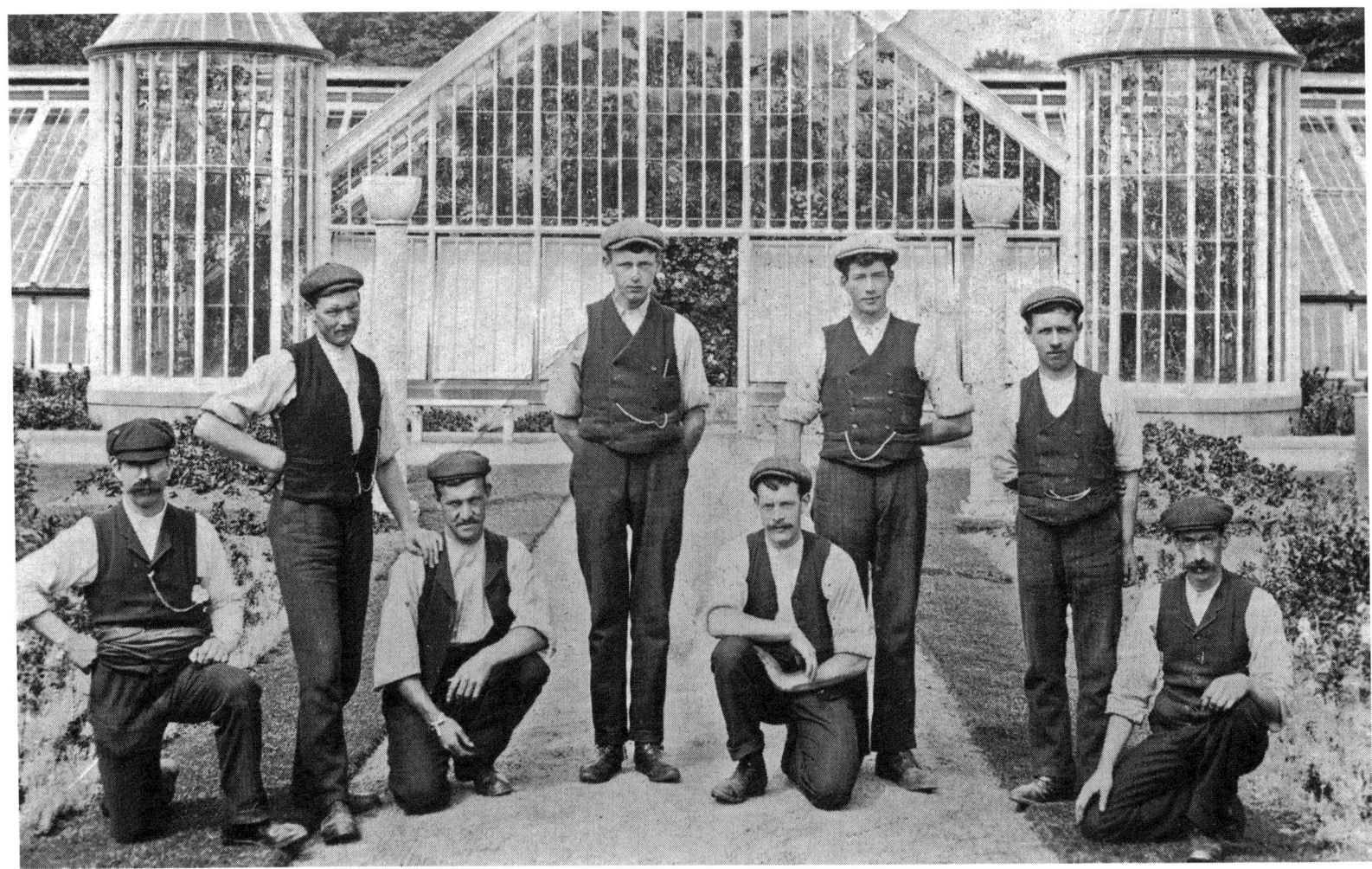

The walled garden was constructed at the same time as the adjacent Home Farm complex c. 1777, and replaced an earlier, square, enclosed garden located immediately to the south-west of Fyvie Castle. The greenhouses were established in the 19th century and each section had a different character. The Ball Green in the northern third contained what was reputed to be the oldest fig house in Scotland. The central section, known as Rhymers How or Haugh, was for the cultivation of fruit, including mulberries, peaches, nectarines and grapes while the southern third, with its outwardly curving low south wall, contained exotic trees, shrubs, paths and seating, and was clearly intended more for leisure than horticultural production.

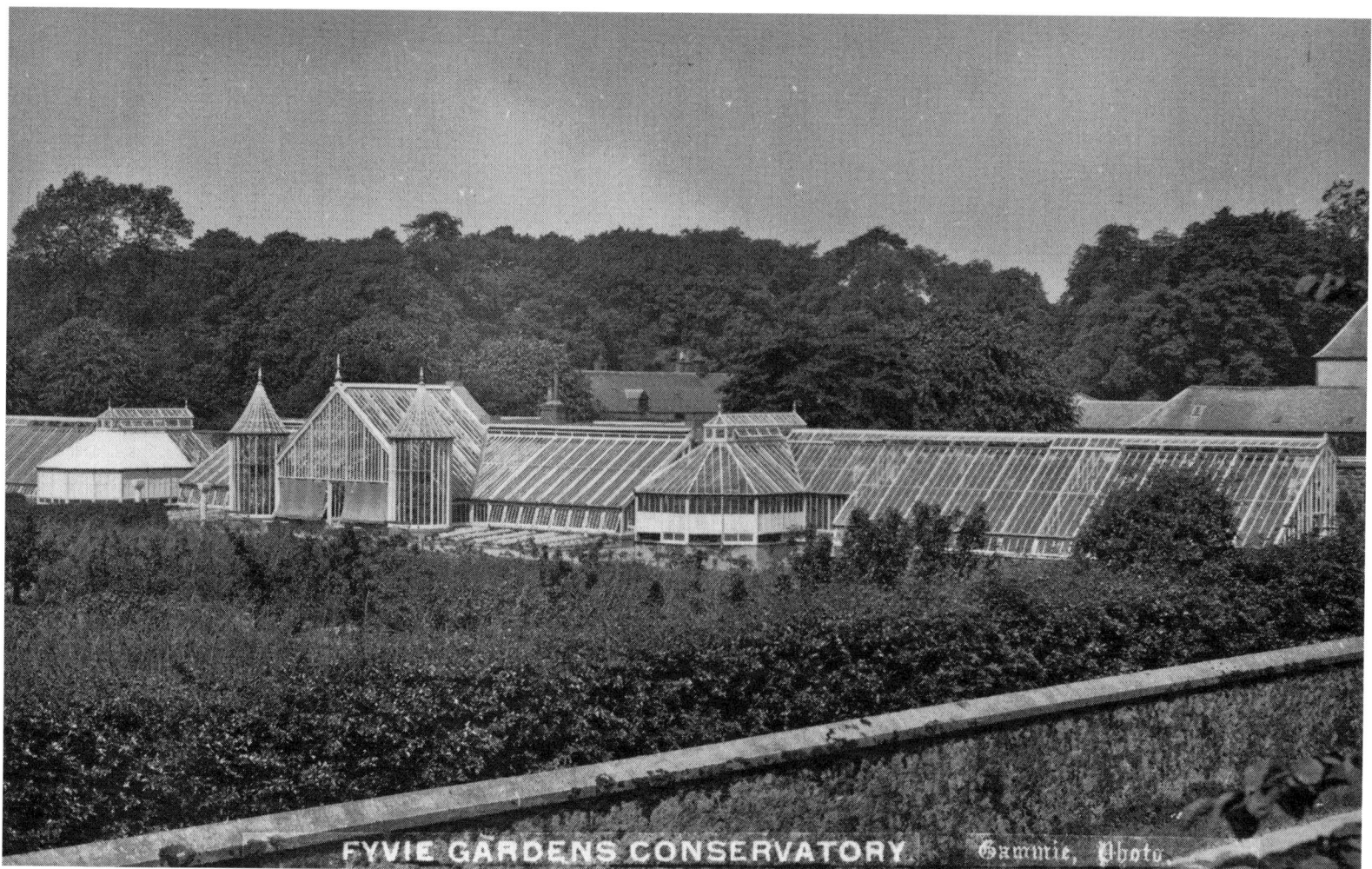
FYVIE GARDENS CONSERVATORY. Gammie, Photo.

In the latter half of the 19th century, the gardens were developed further with the addition of frames and Dutch-lights in the northern section, and the conversion of the principal glasshouse range into an impressive suite of conservatory and hothouse structures. Admired by visitors from the Banffshire Field Club in 1903, the cultivated garden provided work for a team of eight in the earlier 20th century, and remained in use until the outbreak of the Second World War. The walled garden is now a redesigned garden of Scottish fruits and vegetables. Two gardeners currently look after the entire outside gardens and grounds.

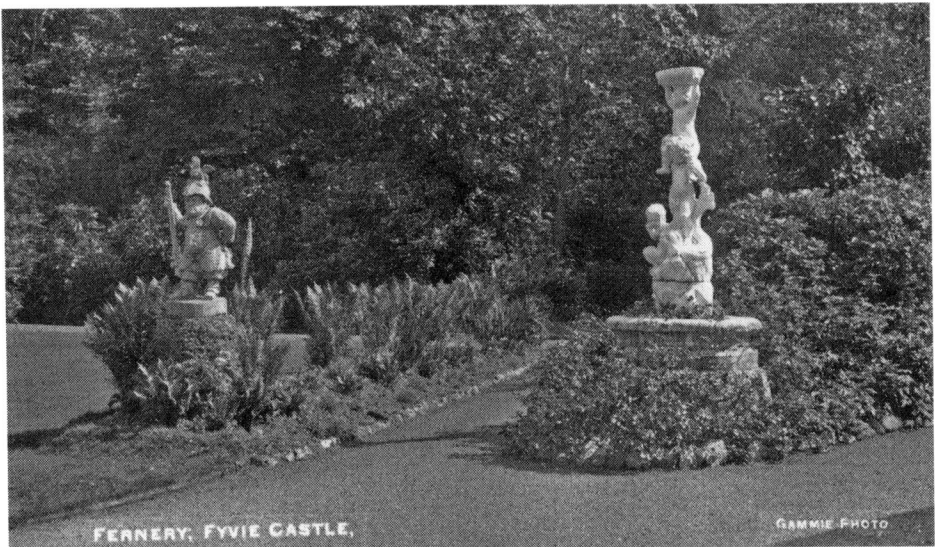
FERNERY, FYVIE CASTLE.

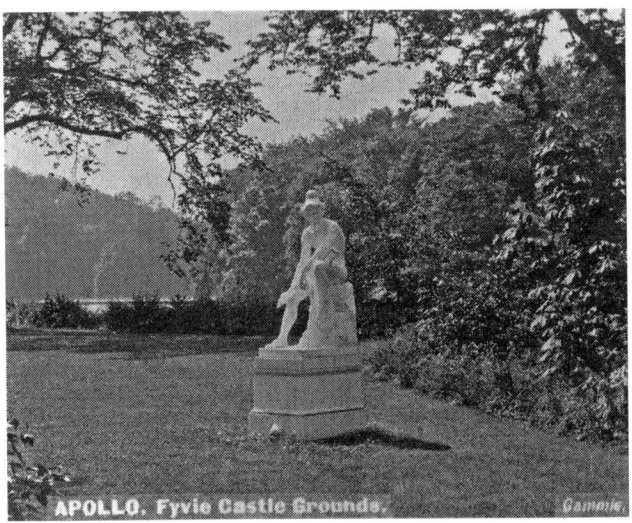
APOLLO, Fyvie Castle Grounds.

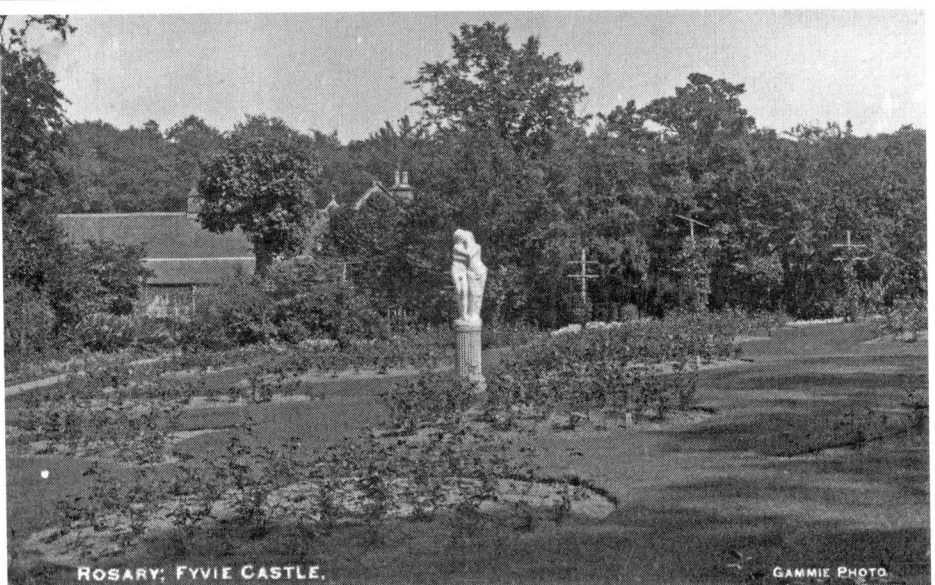
ROSARY, FYVIE CASTLE.

When the National Trust for Scotland acquired the property in 1984, the glasshouses were derelict and much of the garden space was laid to grass. The central portion of the garden was converted for use as car-parking, while the other compartments became the focus of a programme of restoration, launched in 1995. In the northern section, the garden of Scottish fruits and vegetables was designed by Robert Grant, with the geometric layout inspired by motifs found on the plaster ceilings of certain rooms in the castle. Highly commended in two categories in the Aberdeenshire Design Awards 2006, the garden is a well-stocked, colourful and productive area that boasts new statuary and gates, and a very impressive range of carefully documented fruit stocks, including many rare and historic cultivars. Although the important Scottish apple collection was largely destroyed in 2006-07 by rabbits, work is ongoing to rebuild the diverse range of fruits. Immediately to the west of the walled garden is a triangular area of lawns, paths, shrubs and trees, known as the American Garden. Formerly maintained as a rose garden, this garden space was developed following the arrival of the National Trust for Scotland in order to commemorate the historic link between the Forbes-Leith family and the January family in America.

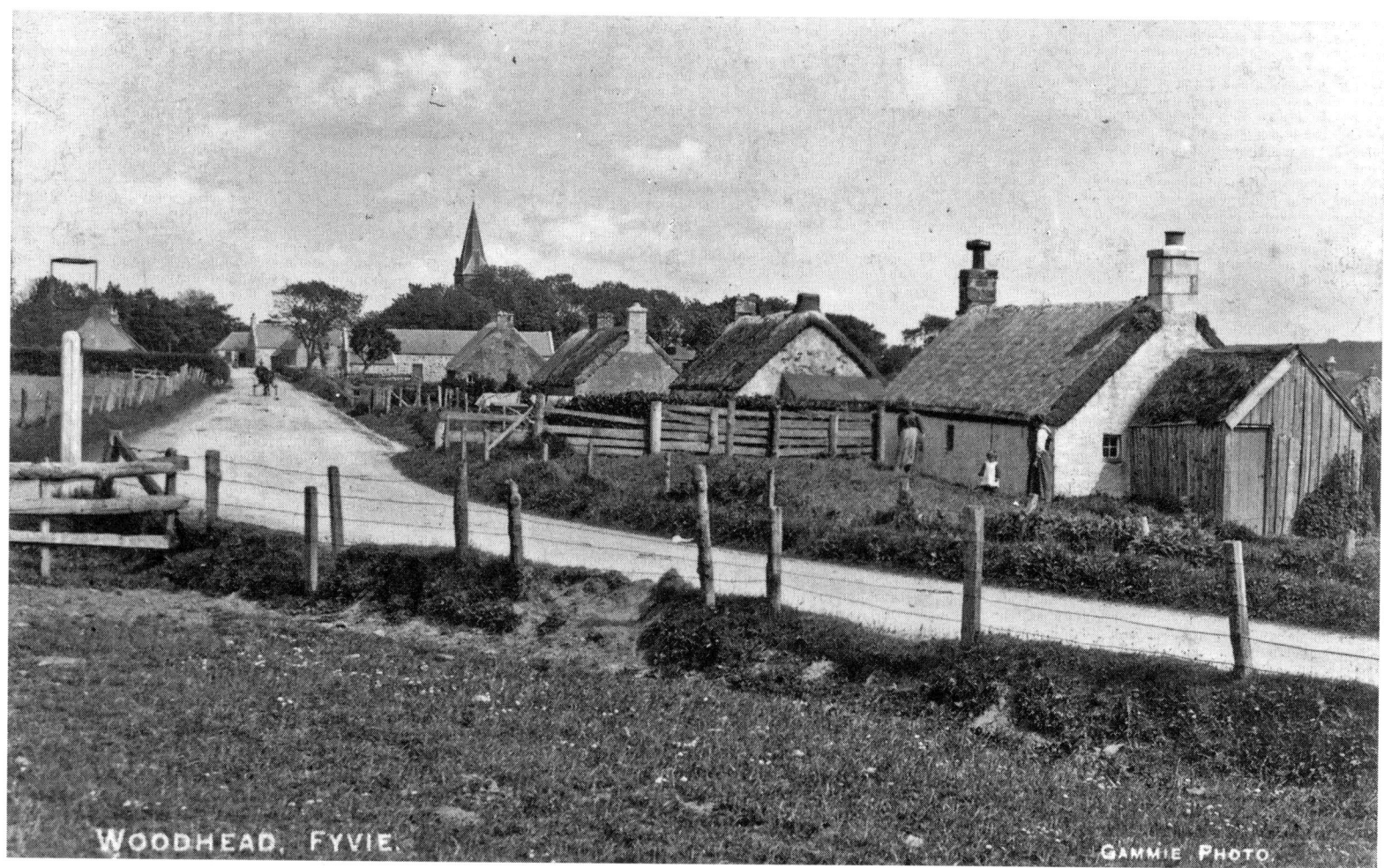

Woodhead, or Woodhead of Fyvie is a small elongated settlement about a mile and a half to the east of Fyvie. It was probably once the main nucleus of settlement in the area and in 1673 it was granted a charter to hold a market. The site is still marked by a cross, although the current Market Cross was erected in 1846. The village of Woodhead had two churches, the Episcopal church and the Free Church. The Free Church and its manse were built in 1843 and lasted just over a century before declining congregation numbers caused its closure in 1959. Afterwards the building was used as a bus garage and latterly as a potato store. On 29th December 1979 an electrical fault caused a fire that lead to the destruction of the building and the loss of £10,000 worth of seed potatoes. The Episcopal All Saints Church, its spire poking above the trees, is still a working church. Until 1919 the land belonged to Haddo House estate.

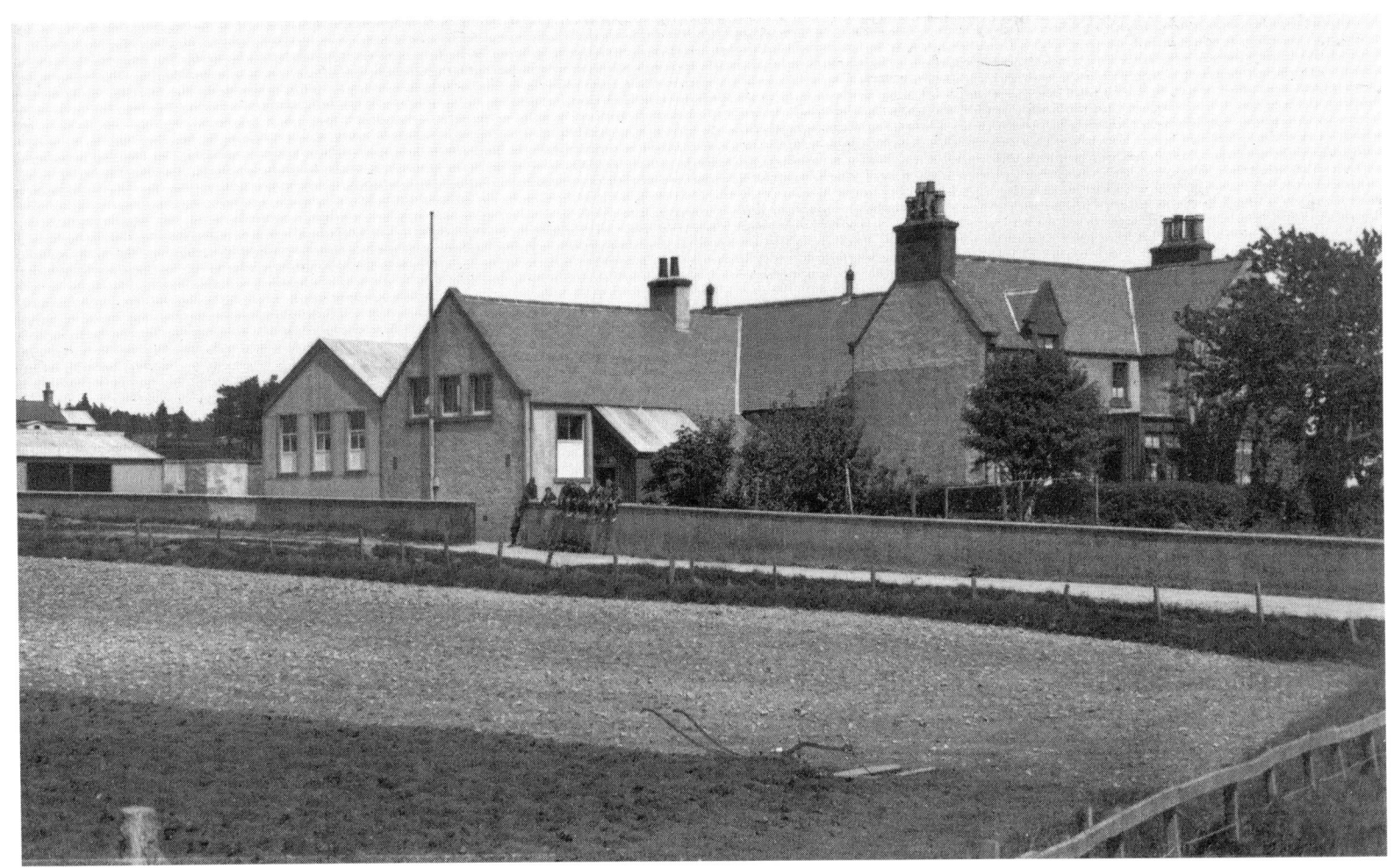

The public school at Woodhead, to the north of the village at Mosslip. Both of the churches in Woodhead had an associated school established before state education was statutory. In 1872 school boards began to appear in Scotland to further public education. The Fyvie School Board was established in 1873. It met in November 1874 and approved £797 for the construction of a public school at Woodhead. The following year they appointed a teacher and considered advertising for a female assistant teacher. The Free Church offered the Board the use of their school for the teacher, assistant teacher and pupils for a sum of £10 yearly. The offer was accepted, and Woodhead Public School remained there until 1876 when it transferred to its new buildings. The school closed in 1966 and its pupils were moved to the new Fyvie School.

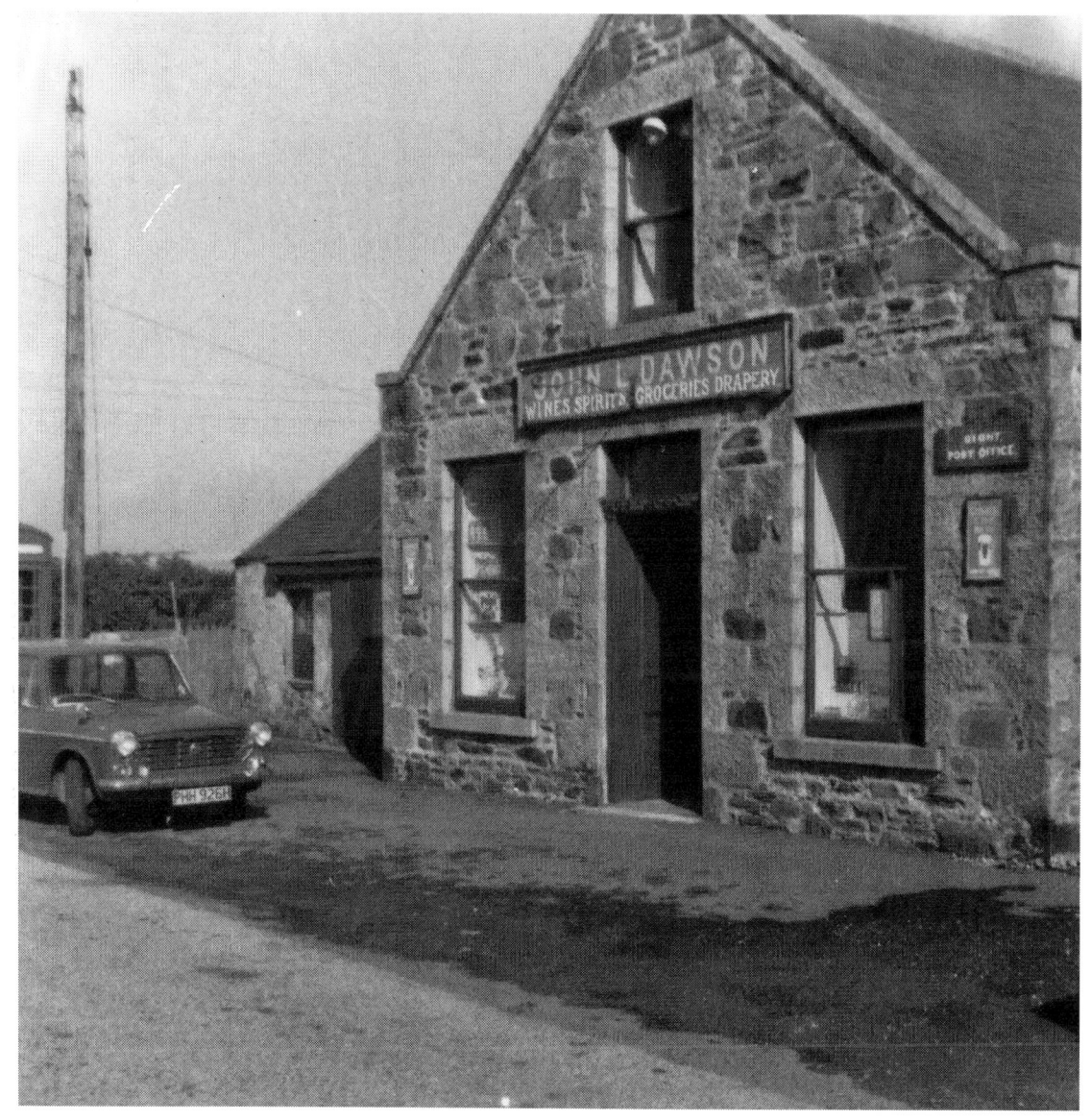

On the road between Woodhead and Methlick was Gight Post Office, photographed in September 1974. The post office and shop were run by John and Margaret Dawson until John's death in 1981. In 1946 they lost their fourteen month old son in horrific circumstance. The toddler crawled unnoticed beneath a lorry making deliveries to the shop. Grimly the child's whereabouts was not discovered until the vehicle moved off and one of its wheels passed over the boy. He was rushed to Aberdeen Sick Children's Hospital where he died. The office's remote rural location made it a target for a break-in on 12th December 1979 when a substantial sum of money was stolen. It was only a few years after Donald Neilsen, armed robber, kidnapper and murderer, had carried out a series of raids on sub-post offices. He was arrested in 1975 but his crimes showed the vulnerability of rural post offices and prompted a string of copycat robberies across Britain.

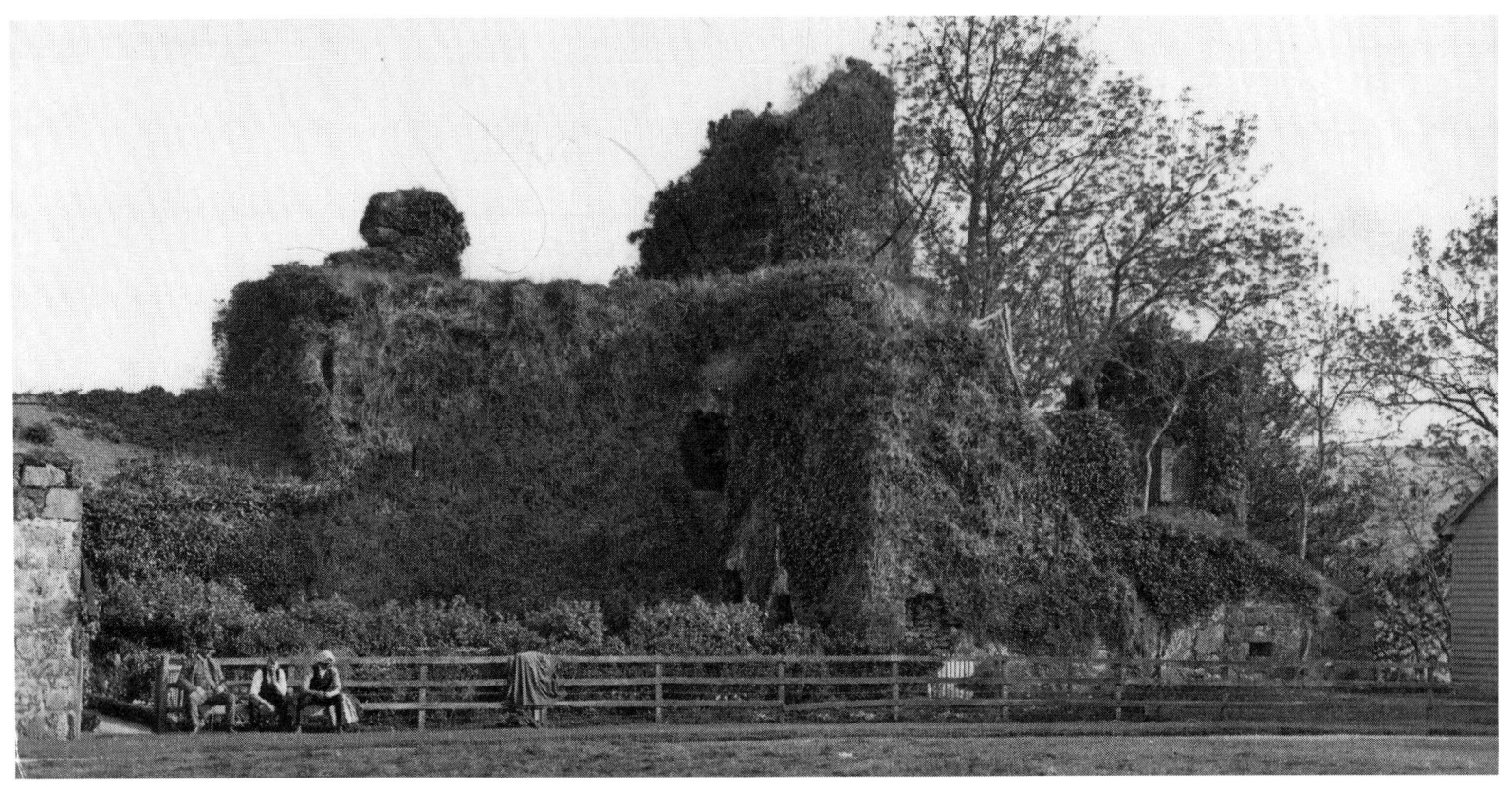

Gight Castle was built in the first half of the 16th century by a branch of the Gordon family, known as the Gordons of Gight. They held the castle from then until the 18th century when the title passed to Catherine Gordon. A 22 year old orphan and wealthy heiress she went to live under the protection of her great uncle Vice Admiral Robert Duff in Bath. It was there that she met Captain John Byron. He was fresh from scandal, after a passionate affair with the married Amelia Osbourne, Lady Carmathen. She became pregnant, eloped with Jack and was divorced by her husband. Six years later with Amelia dead from tuberculosis, Byron was back in England having amassed significant debts, and had his sights set on Catherine Gordon. They married after a whirlwind romance in 1785 on May 12th or 13th she couldn't quite remember. He took her name, in order to claim her estate and in two years he managed to squander the fortune worth £23,500. The castle was sold to George Gordon, 3rd Earl of Aberdeen. His son George Gordon, Lord Haddo, lived there until his death in 1791. He was the castle's last resident after which it became a ruin. With the estate dispersed Jack moved the family to France in 1786 to escape his creditors. Shortly after, Catherine moved back to London where she gave birth to their son, George Gordon Byron. She returned to Aberdeen in 1790 where she took lodgings in Queen Street. George attended Aberdeen Grammar School, and it was there, after the death of his great uncle that the headmaster told him he was now Lord Byron. As he wrote in one of his most famous poems *Don Juan*, which is filled with references to his own life 'But I am half a Scot by birth, and bred / A whole one, and my heart flies to my head.'